BroadStreet Publishing® Group, LLC
Savage, Minnesota, USA
BroadStreetPublishing.com

God Is Love: 365 Devotions from the Gospel of John
Copyright © 2023 Brian Simmons

Written by Brian Simmons with Sara Perry.

9781424566204 (faux leather)
9781424566211 (ebook)

Unless otherwise indicated, all Scripture quotations are from The Passion Translation®. Copyright © 2017, 2018, 2020 by Passion & Fire Ministries, Inc. Used by permission. All rights reserved. ThePassionTranslation.com. Scripture quotations marked NLT are taken from the Holy Bible, New Living Translation, copyright © 1996, 2004, 2015 by Tyndale House Foundation. Used by permission of Tyndale House Publishers, a Division of Tyndale House Ministries, Carol Stream, Illinois 60188. All rights reserved. Scripture quotations marked NCV are taken from the New Century Version®. Copyright © 2005 by Thomas Nelson. Used by permission. All rights reserved.

Stock or custom editions of BroadStreet Publishing titles may be purchased in bulk for educational, business, ministry, fundraising, or sales promotional use. For information, please email orders@broadstreetpublishing.com.

Cover and interior by Garborg Design Works | garborgdesign.com

Printed in China

23 24 25 26 27 5 4 3 2 1

This book is dedicated to the most loving person I know, my wife, Candice. She has loved the widow, the orphan, the outcast, the forgotten, and the prodigal. And she has loved me with the love of Christ.

"Love each other deeply, as much as I have loved you.
For the greatest love of all is a love that sacrifices all."

JOHN 15:12–13

January

## From the Very Beginning

In the beginning the Living Expression was already there. And the Living Expression was with God, yet fully God.

JOHN 1:1

The very beginning of the book of John does not discuss the birth of Jesus. Rather, it discusses his deity. The eternal existence of the Christ is presented at the very start, calling our attention to his essence. He was present in ages past, and he will reign throughout the ages to come. He was with God, being a very part of God himself, at and before the beginning of the universe.

Jesus, the Living Expression of God, is the one who came to lead us to life by illuminating the Father's heart. He revealed the hidden thoughts, plans, and dreams God has for his children. Christ was with God, and he was sent from God to lead us back to him. He came to set the record straight—that God's passionate love for his people meant he would lay down his very life so they could be saved. So we could be saved. What a wonderful God he is.

*YAHWEH, thank you for the power of your gift to us. Jesus Christ, I believe that you were with God at the very beginning, and you came to seek, save, and liberate us in your love. Thank you.*

# In Creativity's Image

Through his creative inspiration
this Living Expression made all things,
for nothing has existence apart from him!

JOHN 1:3

Look out of the closest window. Notice what is around you. Everything that you see came from somewhere. If you see buildings, the materials that make them up were first gathered and fabricated then put together. Notice the way the sun shines. The trees grow even if they stand dormant in the midst of a cold winter.

God is the source of all life. This includes you and me. Nothing has existence apart from him, and nothing thrives without him. We were made in the image of creativity, and that means that each of us is filled with it. We are unique reflections of God's nature. With that in mind, we should celebrate the way we see the world. No one else has our DNA. How boring it would be if we were all the same, and yet so many of us try to shape-shift to blend in. We were born to be ourselves. We come fully alive in the love of Christ, and we don't have to look the same as others to do this.

*Creator, thank you for the freedom I have in you to be myself. Thank you for your love that liberates me, refines me, and heals me. I am yours.*

# Light of Life

A fountain of life was in him, for his life is light for all humanity.
And this Light never fails to shine through darkness—Light that
darkness could not overcome!

JOHN 1:4–5

Every form of life comes from Christ. We are more than bodies; we have spirits and souls. Our whole beings are brought to life in the "Light that darkness could not overcome." Not only does Christ offer us light, but he also is the Light. As we look to him, we are able to see things more clearly. He shines brightly in glory, and he will never diminish. He dwells in radiance, and there are no shadows in his presence.

Bring to Jesus all your worries and cares. Give him your weary hopes and your questions. Look to him and let the light of his presence burst through your own gloom. He is pure light, life, and love. There is ample peace, abundant joy, and pervading hope in him. You were created to dwell in him, to depend on his provision, and to reflect his nature in your own life. It all starts with knowing Christ, who is the Living Expression of the Father. He is the light of life that dispels fear, shame, and the heavy fog of self-doubt.

*Jesus, I look to you today. As I do, burn off all that holds me back from freedom in your love.*

## *Recognizable*

He entered into the world he created, yet the world was unaware.
He came to the people he created—to those who should have
received him, but they did not recognize him.

JOHN 1:10–11

Jesus, the Son of God, came to those he created. He did
not come to strangers but to friends. He was born a
Hebrew, into the very people who should have known him
best. Many did not recognize him, however. The person and
ministry of Jesus Christ challenged their understanding of
who God was, whom he loved, and how he chose to move on
the earth.

We must look at how Christ challenges our own biases.
Are we resistant to his magnanimous mercy that he offers
to all in the same measure? Do we insist that his grace has
limits or conditions? Let's lay down our defenses and allow
ourselves to look with open hearts at the life, ministry,
teachings, and sacrifice of Christ. As we do, we will be able
to recognize his work in our lives and receive more of him.
He offers us so much kindness, grace, strength, and mercy if
we will but receive the truth of who he is.

*Savior, open my spiritual eyes to see who you are and who I
am in light of that. I lay aside my preconceived notions of who
you are and receive you as you are.*

# Children of God

Those who embraced him and took hold of his name he gave
authority to become the children of God!

JOHN 1:12

Each of us has the opportunity to receive the fullness of
God through Christ in our personal lives. We don't have
to jump through hoops to know him. We don't have to look
a certain way, work our tails off, or crack a mysterious code
in order to become a child of God. As we embrace Christ, we
lay hold of his name by believing all that he represents and
by putting into practice what he taught.

The apostle John emphasized the wonderful opportunity
we have to belong to God in his epistle: "Look with wonder at
the depth of the Father's marvelous love that he has lavished
on us! He has called us and made us his very own beloved
children" (1 John 3:1). What indescribable goodness there is
when we embrace Christ as our Savior. As we become more
like him, our lives reflect the beauty of God's character. This
is how we're known as children of the Most High.

*Jesus Christ, I want to live from the expansive mercy of your
heart. I believe that life originates in you and that following
your ways is worth it. Thank you for making a way for me in
your kingdom.*

## Born of God

He was not born by the joining of human parents
or from natural means, or by a man's desire,
but he was born of God.

JOHN 1:13

Just as Jesus was born of God, he offers us the ability to be spiritually reborn as children of God. Jesus was completely human, but he was also fully divine. In him, we find the wholeness—body, soul, and spirit—that we long for. The more we embrace him and his ways, the more holistic our lives become. There is room for us to embrace both the natural and the supernatural, the obvious and the mysterious, in our lives.

God's love is practical, and it meets our needs. God's love is also his very nature. It is greater than anything we can pin down in examples. It is like collecting cups of water to try to understand the ocean. May we be born of God by receiving the fullness that Christ offers. As we get to know him more, we will learn to balance the practicality of his lived-out love in our lives while still remaining students of the mysteries of his kingdom.

*Jesus, in you I have found so much more satisfaction in life than I could have imagined apart from you. I am flesh and bone, and I am spirit. I am born of your kingdom, and I want to represent that fullness in every area of my life.*

# The Living Expression

> The Living Expression became a man and lived among us! We gazed upon his glory, the glory of the One and Only who came from the Father overflowing with tender mercy and truth!
>
> JOHN 1:14

The phrase that the Living Expression "became a man and lived among us" is literally translated "he pitched his tent among us." In the Old Testament, God came down and lived in the tent of the tabernacle when his people were wandering in the wilderness. In the same way, Jesus came to the earth and pitched his tent among us. He is the literal presence of God with us. What a wonderful God he is to come to his people.

Jesus is the full expression of God's character. If we want to know what the Father is truly like, we have to look no further than Christ. He operates in the power and love of God. He is full of purpose, living out the will of the Father. He is motivated by the passion of his heart. God is still overflowing with tender mercy and truth. Come to him and let him wash over you in the refreshing waters of his affection and wisdom.

*Lord, you are worthy of my submission and my trust. I come to you with a heart open to receive from the abundance of your truth and love. Give me greater revelation of the Father as I look to you.*

## Grace upon Grace

From the overflow of his fullness
we received grace heaped upon more grace!

JOHN 1:16

The grace of God is a gift. We cannot earn it, and we cannot disqualify ourselves from it. God freely gives it. There's nothing stopping us from receiving it except perhaps ourselves. The love of God is extravagant. It is infinitely better than we could ever imagine. Out of the fullness of Christ, we are fulfilled. Why, then, would we live as though love and grace are limited resources? They will never run dry.

Consider the many ways you have received "grace heaped upon more grace" from God throughout the years. Make a list and be very specific. Nothing is too small. The God who offered you grace ten years ago or yesterday is the God who offers you grace today. Fill up on his fullness, for there is always more to receive. You don't have to rely on your own fading strength when God offers you more grace. Come to him and receive even more. There is a never-ending supply.

*Gracious God, thank you for the gift of grace heaped upon more grace. I come to you needing a fresh filling. I receive from your fullness, oh Lord. Thank you.*

## Merciful Truth

Moses gave us the Law, but Jesus, the Anointed One,
unveils truth wrapped in tender mercy.

JOHN 1:17

We do not make friends using harsh criticism, and we do not often win hearts through the blunt statement of facts. It is through kindness and care that we win over friends. Paul said in Romans that it is God's extraordinary kindness that melts our hearts and leads us to repentance (2:4). Jesus is truth, and he is tender mercy. We can see both in his life, ministry, and teachings.

We must be sure that we don't lose the tender mercy of Christ when we present truth to others. Whether we are confronting others with how they have wounded us, talking about our differing beliefs, or simply stating our perspective, we should wrap it all up with the tender mercy of Christ. He was humble, and yet he was unflinching in love. What an example to follow. He did not lose himself in the opinions of others. We don't have to agree with others to love them. We can disagree and still be compassionate. We can stand firm on truth and still be kind.

*Anointed One, thank you for your wonderful example of standing in truth but being extremely merciful in relating to others. I want to be just like you.*

# Fullness of God

No one ever before gazed upon the full splendor of God except
his uniquely beloved Son, who is cherished by the Father and held
close to his heart. Now that he has come to us, he has unfolded
the full explanation of who God truly is!

JOHN 1:18

Christ dwelled with God in complete unity at the beginning, and he remained intimately connected to him
when he came to the earth. Jesus was face-to-face with God
as a part of the Godhead since the birth of time. He has no
beginning, and he will have no end. He is the revelation of
the fullness of God's heart to us.

Instead of looking for answers today through others'
words about who God is, spend some time reading through
the account of Jesus' life. Read his words and meditate on
them. Ask the Spirit to reveal his wonderful, expansive goodness to you as you do. Jesus gazed upon the fullness of God's
splendor, and he reveals it to us. There is much more for us
to discover than we have already grasped. May we never stop
learning, growing, and expanding in the wisdom of Christ.

*Glorious Lord, I set aside time right here and now to know you
more. I come with an open heart to receive from your fullness.
Reveal more of yourself to me today.*

# Voice in the Wilderness

John answered them, "I am an urgent, thunderous voice crying out in the desert—clear the way and prepare your hearts for the coming of the Lord YAHWEH!"

JOHN 1:23

John the Baptizer, when the people questioned if he was the Messiah that they had been waiting for, was quick to set the record straight. He was sent to prepare the way for the Anointed One. God had called him to set up camp by the Jordan River, where he implored those he met to change their ways so they would be prepared for an encounter with the Son of God. This is what he did. He was a voice shouting in the wilderness to all who would listen.

John the Baptizer and Jesus were cousins. At some point, it had to have dawned upon John who Jesus truly was. When it did, it changed everything. Just as John's life was completely changed with the revelation of Jesus' identity, so will ours. When we encounter the beautiful truth of who God is through Christ, we are forever transformed. As we do, we will join our voices with those who could not stay silent.

*Jesus, how can I keep quiet about who you are and what you've done? May the message of my life point to you.*

# Lamb of God

The very next day, John saw Jesus coming to him to be baptized, and John cried out, "Look! There he is—God's Lamb! He takes away the sin of the entire world!"

JOHN 1:29

It is not random that John the Baptizer described Jesus as the Lamb of God. He didn't choose an arbitrary animal to describe him. Lambs were used as sacrifices during Passover to cover the sins of each family for the year. Jesus was the Lamb of God who came to take away the sins of the world once and for all. No other sacrifice is needed to cover any of our sins. He is the perfect sacrifice.

Christ willingly set his power aside and humbled himself to be led like an animal in order to be sacrificed in our place. He knew what he was doing. It was not some trick that the Father played. He knew what he was taking on, and he did it willingly. It was love that compelled him. There is no more guilt for those who believe in him. His mission was to take away the sins of the world, and that is what he did. He broke the power of sin's grip over humanity and offers us freedom in his love.

*Lamb of God, thank you for breaking sin's hold over my life. I am liberated in your love.*

## Spirit's Anointing

As he baptized Jesus, he proclaimed these words: "I see the Spirit of God appear like a dove descending from the heavenly realm and landing upon him—and it remained on him!"

JOHN 1:32

The dove is a clear sign of the Spirit of God. The Spirit's anointing was upon Jesus as soon as John baptized him, and it never left him. Jesus came to save us, but he also came to bring the fullness of life to us. This includes, in large part, the fullness of the Spirit.

The writer of John also wrote that "the Spirit, who is truth, confirms this with his testimony" (1 John 5:6). The witness of Jesus Christ as the Anointed One is testified by the Spirit. This means that we can know the power of this testimony within our own fellowship with the Spirit. Those who believe in Christ have also been given the Holy Spirit as helper, teacher, and companion. The same Spirit who rested on Jesus is the Spirit who dwells with us. Do we take this for granted, or do we know, embrace, and honor this privilege?

*Anointed One, thank you for your Spirit that dwells with me today. I ask for the testimony of your Spirit to reveal your truth in deeper ways.*

# What Do You Want?

Jesus turned around and saw they were following him and asked, "What do you want?" They responded, "Rabbi (which means, Master Teacher), where are you staying?"

JOHN 1:38

Jesus' question to those who were following him was not an annoyed, "Why are you following me?" It was an earnest question. "What do you want?" These men Jesus was speaking to were Andrew and Simon, whom he would later call Peter. They would become two of his disciples. Think about your own life and when you first encountered Jesus. What did you want from him then?

It is important to know our motivations. Jesus knows this as well as anyone else. There are no right or wrong answers here. Think about what you wanted when you first began following Jesus. Was it simply to know him more? Whatever the answer, note it. Now consider what you want from him now. How has your motivation changed? Expectations in relationships change over time. It is not a bad thing to recognize a difference. Still, consider what it is that you truly want from him, and answer his question today.

*Jesus, I'm so glad that relationship with you is fluid and that I can answer you honestly. Speak to my heart and fellowship with me heart-to-heart.*

## Spiritual Sight

> "I prophesy to you eternal truth: From now on, you all will see
> an open heaven and gaze upon the Son of Man like a stairway
> reaching into the sky with the messengers of God climbing up
> and down upon him!"
>
> JOHN 1:51

Jesus had just finished telling Nathanael about himself, having never met him, and Nathanael was in awe because of it. However, Jesus didn't stop with what Nathanael already knew. He said to him, "You will experience even more impressive things than that" (v. 50). He prophesied his future—that Nathanael would see the Son of Man as a bridge between God and his people.

Jesus Christ is our Mediator and our bridge. He came to be the link between heaven and earth, and he remains that to this day. We can also experience what Nathanael experienced with our spiritual eyes opened by the Spirit. We don't have to settle for what we already have experienced or know. So much more is ahead of us, even more impressive things than we have known.

*Jesus, I long to know you more. Open my eyes to see your glory.*

# The Start of Something Big

Mary...asked, "They have no wine; can't you do something about it?" Jesus replied, "My dear one, don't you understand that if I do this, it will change nothing for you, but it will change everything for me! My hour of unveiling my power has not yet come."

JOHN 2:2–4

Mary clearly knew that Jesus had power and anointing to perform miracles before she asked Jesus to intervene in this dilemma. Though the limits of this world are reached time and again, the resources of Christ's kingdom are limitless. For Mary, little would change if he performed the miracle, but for Jesus, everything about his public ministry would change.

In the end, Jesus chose to turn water into wine and went on to astound the master of the ceremonies. This was the first time that a large number of people witnessed Jesus' power. He was willing to honor his mother's request, knowing that it would transform his life and ministry. Sometimes a push from someone else is what propels us into a new season even before we had originally planned. That doesn't mean it's wrong!

*Jesus, your life gives so much instruction for how to honor others while also asserting our own agency. When I am afraid of change, help me to step forward when the opportunity presents itself.*

## Water to Wine

When he tasted the water that had become wine, the master of ceremonies was impressed…He called the bridegroom over and said to him, "Every host serves his best wine first, until everyone has had a cup or two, then he serves the cheaper wine. But you, my friend, you've reserved the most exquisite wine until now!"

JOHN 2:9–10

The first recorded miracle of Jesus in the book of John was not meeting a need or healing a body. To some it may actually seem superfluous. Jesus set a precedent with his first miracle; he showered his friends with good things. It was with joyful abandon that Jesus turned water into wine. The bridegroom went from certain humiliation, having run out of wine, to having the best wine to offer his guests. What a gracious gift this was!

Think about a time when you had nothing, having run out of your own resources, to being blessed beyond belief. How have the joyful offerings of Jesus transformed your life? Maybe you find yourself on the edge of hope today, wondering if God would move on your behalf simply for the joy that giving good gifts brings him. Dare to ask him for what you want today.

*Jesus, I am astounded by your wonderful kindness toward your friends. Thank you for caring about what we care about. May wonder abound as you move in marvelous love on my behalf.*

# *First of Many*

This miracle in Cana was the first of the many extraordinary miracles Jesus performed in Galilee that revealed his glory, and his disciples believed in him.

JOHN 2:11

The miracles of Jesus were demonstrations of his power and authority. They each display God's love for us. When we take time to ponder the ways of God revealed through the mighty acts of Jesus, our hearts grow in the knowledge of God's nature. We cannot look at these things and remain the same.

What God has already done is representative of what is to come. God is always moving in mighty mercy. God has not stopped working miracles through his Spirit. Jesus told his disciples that those who follow him in faith would do even greater things than they witnessed him do (John 14:12). This promise stands as strong and true today as it did when Jesus spoke it at first. He moves in signs and wonders that reveal his glory and cause people to believe in the Son of God, and he does it through those who believe.

*Holy Spirit, move through my life in power as I submit to your ways. I do not live for my own satisfaction alone. I live for you.*

## Flipping Tables

Jesus...drove out every one of them and their animals from the courtyard of the temple, and he kicked over their tables filled with money, scattering it everywhere! And he told the merchants, "Get these things out of here! Don't you dare commercialize my Father's house!"

JOHN 2:15–16

God is full of extravagant grace. We see this so clearly through the miracle of turning the water into wine at the wedding banquet. God is also full of extravagant truth and justice. These are not mutually exclusive. When Jesus saw that the sellers at the market were greedy, taking advantage of the people they sold to, he was outraged.

There is no room for corruption in the house of God. How much of this has become so commonplace that we just accept it as part of the way things are done? Jesus would not stand for it, and we don't have to play along to appease the corrupt. Apathy is not a fruit of the Spirit. There is a time for extravagant grace, and there is a time to flip tables. When we witness corruption in the church, we don't have to question which response is appropriate. Truth and justice matter.

*Jesus, thank you for exposing corruption within your Father's house. I see now that it is appropriate to call for justice within your church. You stand for the vulnerable and oppressed, and so will I.*

# Prophetic Declaration

They failed to understand that Jesus was speaking of the "temple" of his body. The disciples remembered his prophecy after Jesus rose from the dead, and believed both the Scripture and what Jesus had said.

JOHN 2:21–22

God is with us in the present, and he meets us in fullness here. He gives us wisdom to guide us, grace to strengthen us, and love to cover us. When he speaks to us and it doesn't quite come together in our understanding, it may be because God is giving us a word for the future. We should note these instead of ignoring them.

Many times, when the Lord speaks to us, he speaks of what is to come. Jesus was preparing those who listened to him for his resurrection, even at the beginning of his ministry. As proof that he had the authority of God, Jesus told the religious leaders, "Destroy this temple, and I will raise it up again in three days" (v. 19). Later, after Jesus rose from the dead, his disciples would remember this prophecy, and it would strengthen their faith. So is our faith strengthened as God reminds us of his prophetic declarations in our lives.

*Jesus, as I spend time with you thinking over my life and your words over me, bring to mind what you have already fulfilled. You are so very faithful.*

## Growing Following

While Jesus was at the Passover Feast, the number of his followers began to grow, and many gave their allegiance to him because of all the miraculous signs they had seen him doing!

JOHN 2:23

When Jesus moved in mighty miracles, many believed in him. Perhaps you have experienced a miracle of your own or witnessed one in the life of a loved one or close friend. What effect did that have on you? Consider whether your response led to lasting transformation in your thinking, your lifestyle, or your relationships.

A miraculous sign is enough to get the attention and accolades of many, but that attention may not last. Jesus' mission was not to win the favor of the masses. It was also not to appease the powerful, either within the local government or in the religious order. Jesus is greater than any human system. He did not need the approval of people to do what he set out to do. His identity was rooted and grounded in his relationship with the Father, and that never changed. No matter how much or how little favor we have among our peers, our true identity is rooted in the love of Christ.

*Jesus, your wonders draw the masses, and I'm no different. I want more than just your signs, though. I want to know you.*

# Fickle Hearts

Jesus did not yet entrust himself to them,
because he knew how fickle human hearts can be.

JOHN 2:24

It was wisdom that kept Jesus from getting caught up in the attention he was drawing from so many. He knew that a person could sing his praises one day and turn from him the next. Some are won over by how impressive a person seems, but Jesus knew that those who truly desired to know God would stick around. Jesus was not flashy, and though many turned to follow him, he knew that some would not stay.

When we gain quick favor with lots of people, we shouldn't trust ourselves to them. There is a reason why Jesus picked twelve disciples, twelve close friends to pour into and trust. He ministered to all who came to him, but he did not entrust his own heart to everyone. We can learn from his example and allow ourselves time to build bridges of trust in relationships.

*Jesus, I know that there is a lot that I am fickle about, but I don't ever want you to be one of those things. I want to know you more deeply than surface knowledge. May we build even more trust between us today.*

# He Can't Be Fooled

He needed no one to tell him about human nature,
for he fully understood what man was capable of doing.

JOHN 2:25

God cannot be fooled by humanity. He sees through empty promises and cannot be tricked into believing something that is false. Even when we err in judgment, Jesus never does. When he walked this earth, he fully understood what humans were capable of doing, and he has that full understanding still.

There is wisdom in staying grounded in reality. Hope is not divorced from the harsh realities of this life. It is an approach to the unknown that grounds us in God's goodness. We can hold the tension of optimism without dismissing the flaws within our nature. When we truly trust that Jesus can't be fooled, we can trust him to guide us through this life. Life won't be perfect, but it will be good. He doesn't expect perfection from us but openhearted surrender.

*Lord Jesus, thank you that there is no pressure to be perfect in your eyes. You already know what human nature is like, and you cannot be surprised by it. Even so, I surrender to you and follow your ways. Lead me in your love.*

## Reborn

Jesus answered, "Nicodemus, listen to this eternal truth: Before a person can even perceive God's kingdom, they must first experience a rebirth...I speak an eternal truth: Unless you are born of water and the Spirit, you will never enter God's kingdom."

JOHN 3:3, 5

Nicodemus was a Pharisee and member of the ruling council where Jesus was ministering. He had questions for Jesus, and he came to him discreetly to ask them. Jesus was gracious with him, giving his time and attention to teach this religious leader.

Jesus turned Nicodemus' understanding of the kingdom on its head. The kingdom of God is not something we buy or earn, and it isn't something that we can dissect in order to find. We must be born again—of the Spirit—to experience it. We need the Spirit of God to bring us out of our safe yet small understanding into the realm of his expansive mercy. We cannot do any of it without God. How humbling and yet how wonderful this news is.

*Lord, thank you for the power of your Spirit that offers new life. Usher me into the expanse of your kingdom, to places I have yet to go. I am yours.*

# Led by the Spirit

"The Spirit-Wind blows as it chooses. You can hear its sound,
but you don't know where it came from or where it's going.
So it is the same with those who are Spirit-born!"

JOHN 3:8

The Holy Spirit contains so much mystery. We cannot pin him down just as we cannot pin down the wind. We see the effects of the wind, and we also can recognize how the Spirit moves in our lives and on the earth. When we are led by the Spirit, there may be things we cannot explain, and that's okay. The fruit of his presence is peace, joy, love, kindness, patience, faith, strength of spirit, and gentleness (see Galatians 5:22–23). If we are led by these, we are led by the Spirit.

We must be willing to embrace more than logic in our lives. We must be willing to admit that there is more at work within the world than we can pin down in our understanding. This is not to say that we have no agency. How we live matters, and what we choose also matters. As we live with the values of the kingdom as our guideposts, the Spirit leads us. There's no need to resist the pull of his extravagant love as it moves us out of our comfort zones.

*Spirit, move in my heart and lead me today.*

## Eternal Truths

"I speak eternal truths about things I know,
things I've seen and experienced—
and still you don't accept what I reveal."

JOHN 3:11

Jesus was speaking Teacher-to-teacher as he responded to Nicodemus in this verse. Instructors can only teach what they themselves have already learned. Jesus was teaching truths that he had seen and experienced. We already know he was present with God before the beginning of time. He had every authority to speak on creation, humanity, and the kingdom of his Father.

Do we truly trust that Jesus knows what he is talking about? Do we accept what he has revealed? When the mysteries of his teachings feel too nebulous, let's come to him and ask him for clarification. We can dig for more understanding. We can press into his presence and bring our questions and doubts with us. He can handle it all! As he speaks his truth, let's remember who he is: the Eternal One. In him, through him, and because of him, all things live, move, and have their being, and this includes you and me.

*Eternal One, thank you for your patience with us. I come to you with all my questions today, and I am open to receive all that you offer.*

# Natural and Heavenly Revelation

"If you're unable to believe what I've told you about the natural realm, what will you do when I begin to unveil the heavenly realm?"

JOHN 3:12

There are levels to our faith, and it builds upon the foundation that is laid. Jesus is the Way, the Truth, and the Life. If we don't believe what he says about how to live, how will we react when his kingdom is revealed? We must submit ourselves to his leadership in this natural realm, applying his wisdom to our lives in very practical ways. If we don't, then we will not recognize or embrace the heavenly revelation he offers.

It is not either-or when it comes to the limits of this world and the limitlessness of God's kingdom. It is both-and. Our capacity has limits. But when we learn to practice mutuality, to embrace the rhythms of nature, and to live out the mercy of Christ, we make room for the heavenly abundance of his kingdom to invade our lives.

*Jesus, I know your wisdom is both practical and more intricate and vast than I can understand. I will put into practice what you teach, and I trust you to offer more as I grow in my capacity to receive.*

# Invitation to Receive

"Here is the way God loved the world—he gave his only, unique Son as a gift. So now everyone who believes in him will never perish but experience everlasting life."

JOHN 3:16

John 3:16 sums up the central message of John's gospel. Jesus, the Son of God, is a walking, talking demonstration of God's love that brings the light and life of salvation to the world. Christ, the One who was with the Father at the beginning and who is God, came to this earth as a gift to us. He offers eternal light, life, and love to all who look to him.

Has your belief in Christ transformed your life? Think about the last time you meditated on the freedom that Christ has given you. If you have withheld any part of your heart from him, today is the perfect day to surrender to his overwhelming love. He is better than you can imagine! He does not liberate you only to bind you with unrealistic expectations. His love is light—it expands and is constantly expanding. His love is energizing—it infuses everything it touches with his grace and strength. There is always more to receive from his never-ending love, so don't hesitate today.

*Christ Jesus, you are the Light of the World, and I come alive in your radiant presence. Love me to life in unprecedented ways as I welcome you into my life, body and soul, community and relationships.*

## *Rescuer and Redeemer*

"God did not send his Son into the world to judge and condemn the world, but to be its Savior and rescue it!"

JOHN 3:17

The religious people of Jesus' day were awaiting the Messiah. They were expecting him to be a political leader, freeing the Jewish people from Roman rule and oppression. Jesus did not come to save or overturn earthly systems. He came to bring eternal salvation, opening the way to have uninterrupted connection with God and to enjoy everlasting life with him in heaven.

As long as our hopes are set on earthly systems, we will be disappointed. In fact, we may be offended by the actual work of God in the world, as the Pharisees were. The Father cares much more about people than he does institutions. Jesus turned the world, as his followers knew it, upside down. He is Rescuer and Redeemer, and his ways are far better than any nation, government, or council.

*Jesus, thank you for coming to show us what the Father is really like. Continue to refine my expectations and ideals in the truth of your love.*

## No Condemnation

"Now there is no longer any condemnation for those who believe in him, but the unbeliever already lives under condemnation because they do not believe in the name of the only Son of God."

JOHN 3:18

In Christ there is no condemnation. These words are echoed by Paul in Romans 8:1: "The case is closed. There remains no accusing voice of condemnation against those who are joined in life-union with Jesus, the Anointed One." Simply put, those who are found in Christ cannot be condemned.

What a liberating truth this is. When you come to the Lord, laying your heart and life bare before him, he welcomes you. As you make him the leader over your life, submitting yourself to him, he wipes your slate clean before the Father. King David put it this way in his psalm of praise: "Farther than from a sunrise to a sunset—that's how far you've removed our guilt from us" (Psalm 103:12). What a reason to rejoice!

*Son of God, thank you for becoming my liberation and for offering me the incredible gift of guiltlessness before God. There is nothing better than that! I believe that you are the Way, the Truth, and the Life. Lead me even deeper into your liberating love.*

# Light of God

"Here is the basis for their judgment: The Light of God has now come into the world, but the people loved darkness more than the Light, because they want the darkness to conceal their evil."

JOHN 3:19

What does your heart long for more than anything else? Think about the things you are willing to sacrifice time and money for. What are the things that always have priority in your life? As you get an idea of where your priorities are, you might also consider the values you want to live by. Even if you see where your lifestyle does not match your hopes, you can adjust those things today.

Step into the Light of God and allow him to reveal what is already so clear to him. There is love in his light. There is peace. There is joy. There is freedom. There is hope. He will not condemn you, and he will not turn you away. If there is dread in your heart at the thought of God seeing you, know that there is a warm embrace of loving-kindness awaiting you as you turn your attention to him. Even his correction is laced with kindness. Stand in his light, and you will have nothing to hide.

*Gracious God, I won't hedge in the shadows today. I step into your light, and I welcome your presence. Give me greater revelation of your goodness as I do.*

February

# Fully Exposed

"The wicked hate the Light and try to hide from it,
for the Light fully exposes their lives."

JOHN 3:20

In the light of Christ, everything is exposed. Those who do corrupt and hateful things in the name of God, of power, or of greed cannot hide in the shadows forever. They will be fully exposed in the Light. We should not be so naive as to think that all who claim to know Christ and live for him are people of integrity. It is not our place to judge others, but when dark deeds are exposed, we should deal with them and not cover them up.

It is wise to live without anything to hide. Authenticity is a good way to go about relating to others. God knows our hearts, and he deals with us each accordingly. What does this mean in community? Our directive from Christ is to love God and to love others the way we love ourselves. If "others" does not include everyone, we have some work to do in letting the light of Christ transform us.

*Light of God, shine on me today. Your light is life-giving, and it reveals all for what it truly is. It dispels fear and confusion, and it offers clarity. I am yours, Lord, and I submit to you.*

## Into the Light

"Those who love the truth will come into the Light, for the Light will reveal that it was God who produced their fruitful works."

JOHN 3:21

When we live in the light of God's truth, our lives become fruitful fields that reflect the Spirit's work. Living in the light of Christ means more than just believing that he is the Son of God. It requires the submission of our lives, putting his teachings into practice in our interactions with others. It means that we surrender our offenses to him and, instead, walk in the ways of his love.

Loving the truth actually requires practicing the truth. If we truly love something, we will do more than pay it lip service. We make sacrifices, giving our time, attention, and resources to it. Loving the truth that Christ revealed leads us to prioritize it even over our own preferences. Rather than depleting our lives, the light of Christ infuses us with an abundance of nourishing fruit. What a wonderful and skilled gardener he is.

*Jesus, thank you for the work that you do in my life. I yield to your life-giving light. I welcome your truth. Have your way with me.*

# No Need to Compare

They went to John and asked him, "Teacher, are you aware that the One you told us about at the crossing place—he's now baptizing crowds larger than yours. People are flocking to him!" John answered them, "A person cannot receive even one thing unless God bestows it."

JOHN 3:26–27

When we compare ourselves to others, we can fall into the trap of competing with others out of fear that someone else's success means there will be less for us. We do not work from a deficit in the kingdom of God but rather from a place of abundance. The table has room for everyone. There is space enough for our own victories as well as the victories of others.

John the Baptizer's disciples may have felt threatened by the ministry of Jesus, but John did not. He knew that God's anointing rests wherever he bestows it. In the same way, we can honor the successes of others while refusing to see our worth through the lens of others' approval. When we tend to our giftings and keep our focus on what is ours to do, we can let go of the need to compare ourselves to others.

*Teacher, thank you for the abundance of your love, grace, and presence. I have all I need in you today.*

# Friend of the Bridegroom

"He is the Bridegroom, and the bride belongs to him. I am the friend of the Bridegroom who stands nearby and listens with great joy to the Bridegroom's voice. Because of his words, my joy is complete and overflows!"

JOHN 3:29

John the Baptizer never said he was the Messiah. He always acted as a forerunner, and he knew his place. When his disciples questioned him about what he thought of Jesus' growing following, John did not hesitate in his response. He painted the picture of Jesus as Bridegroom and himself as the friend of the Bridegroom. The words of Jesus actually brought him tremendous joy.

What a different reaction this was from the Pharisees. They were troubled by the words of Jesus and the favor he was gaining with the people. John the Baptizer knew that Jesus was the Messiah, and it was his overwhelming joy to witness his rise. Are we good friends—not only to Jesus but also to those we love? When we rejoice in their successes, mourn in their losses, and support them as they need it, we know that we are good friends.

*Jesus, I want to be a good friend. Help me to approach friendships the same way that John the Baptizer approached you.*

## *Necessary to Decrease*

> "It is necessary for him to increase
> and for me to decrease."
>
> JOHN 3:30

John the Baptizer was the one who prepared the way for the coming of the Lord. Isaiah 40:3 prophesied his role: "A thunderous voice cries out in the wilderness: 'Prepare the way for YAHWEH's arrival! Make a highway straight through the desert for our God!'" Mark 1:4 says it even more clearly: "John the Baptizer was the messenger who appeared in the wilderness, preaching a baptism of repentance for the complete cancellation of sins."

Having fulfilled his role, John knew that he had to pass the baton, so to speak. It was time for Jesus' influence to increase while John's own decreased. At times, especially during transition, holding on to our previous influence may hinder what needs to happen. We cannot hold on to old patterns when new seasons are upon us. May we recognize the times when we must decrease so another can increase, letting go and embracing the transition instead of resisting the change.

*Lord, the more of you I get to know, the more I realize that life is cyclical and change is not a threat. I yield to your leadership even when it means I am less prominent than I once was.*

# Highest Realm of Knowledge

"The one who is from the earth belongs to the earth and speaks from the natural realm. But the One who comes from above is above everything and speaks of the highest realm of all!"

JOHN 3:31

John the Baptizer knew that Jesus' wisdom was far greater than his own. Do we also recognize this? We can only reveal what we know, and for each of us, our knowledge has limits. Jesus, the Son of God, was more than human; he was and is divine. He intrinsically knows what we cannot imagine. Why wouldn't we trust him when he has greater wisdom than anyone else?

We cannot make the power of God's love fit our small understanding of it. We must resist the pull to limit God's grace. Jesus taught from the highest realm of all. Our understanding of the expansiveness of his kingdom grows as we put his ways into practice in our own lives. There is more freedom, more grace, more forgiveness, more peace, more joy—you name it—in the reality of his realm. May our understanding increase as we dive into the sea of his mercy.

*Jesus, with you there is no beginning, and there will never be an end. The capacity of your kingdom has no limit. I want to grow in your wisdom, past the limits of my knowledge.*

# Fullness of the Spirit

"The One whom God has sent to represent him will speak the words of God, because God has poured out upon him the fullness of the Holy Spirit without limitation."

JOHN 3:34

Jesus was the first instance of the Holy Spirit being poured out upon a person without measure. The Holy Spirit was at home in him, and he operated in the fullness of his giftings. Jesus was human, but he was also divine. Jesus came to break every barrier that keeps us from the fullness of his life, and the Spirit is a huge part of that.

Through faith in Christ, we are offered the abundance of the Spirit's life within us. We have so much more to experience than we have yet known. Colossians 2:10 says that "our own completeness is now found in him. We are completely filled with God as Christ's fullness overflows within us." We are filled with God through our faith in Christ and his Spirit that overflows within us. There is unbroken fellowship that offers us full access to God at all times. We need not operate on empty when God offers us strength from the limitless abundance of his very being.

*Spirit, thank you for making your home in me. I yield to your leadership, and I open wide to receive more of you today.*

# Eternal Life

"The Father loves his Son so much that he has given all things into his hands. Those who trust in the Son possess eternal life; those who don't obey the Son will not see life, and God's anger will rise up against them."

JOHN 3:35–36

Everything—all things, all authority, and all people—has been given into the hands of Christ. No one has more right or authority than he does. This is good news for those of us who follow and trust him. He cannot be fooled, overrun by evil, or manipulated. What he does, he does freely and with full agency.

Jesus is the Way, the Truth, and the Life. He offers eternal life to all who trust in him. Trusting in him requires more than a cognitive belief. Obeying him shows that we truly believe that what he says is true. When we follow Jesus, we will not avoid pain, disappointment, or all sorts of troubles in this life. We will, however, know his comfort, his presence, and his power in the midst of it. Most of all, we will experience the glory of dwelling in his kingdom forever.

*Jesus, I believe that you hold more authority than anyone in this world. I trust your intentions more than I trust in the powerful people around me. You are better than any other, and I give you my allegiance in every part of my life.*

# News Spreads

The news quickly reached the Jewish religious leaders known
as the Pharisees that Jesus was drawing greater crowds of
followers coming to be baptized than John.

JOHN 4:1

Jesus' fame was growing after his first two miracles. His
number of followers was growing by the day, exceeding
the numbers that were going to John for baptism. This was
concerning to the Jewish religious leaders. They saw Jesus as
a radical, and they probably felt threatened by his influence.
Perhaps they were even a bit jealous.

Whatever their feelings, we know that they were
offended. Jesus would not have left the area so abruptly (v.
3) if he did not sense that they would try to trap him there.
Good news travels far and fast. We cannot control how
people will receive it, but that's not our responsibility. Our
obligation is to keep walking in the way that Christ has laid
for us and to listen to his leading when it's time to move on.

*Lord, I'm so glad we are not built to micromanage people's
reactions or thoughts toward us. You certainly didn't, and
you are the example we are to look to. Give me strength to
keep going in what you have given me to do even when others
disagree.*

## A Thirsty Savior

> Wearied by his long journey, he sat on the edge of Jacob's well, and sent his disciples into the village to buy food, for it was already afternoon. Soon a Samaritan woman came to draw water. Jesus said to her, "Give me a drink."
>
> JOHN 4:6–8

Jesus' thirst was not only for water from the well; it was also for this woman's company. To be sure, Jesus experienced natural thirst. This interaction, however, was about far more than meeting a physical need. It was an opening into true connection. Jesus may have started out focused on his thirst, but that changed as their conversation began.

Jesus is as thirsty for your devotion as he was for the Samaritan woman's. It doesn't matter your history, your questions, or anything else. He longs for your company. He wants you to know him as well as he already knows you. He offers you the living water that satisfies. Are you willing to quench the Savior's thirst even as he offers you the refreshing water of his love?

*Savior, you have my heart and my devotion. I offer you all that I am, every part of me, because you are so loving, so kind, and so trustworthy.*

# An Unexpected Interaction

She replied, "Why would a Jewish man ask a Samaritan woman for a drink of water?"

JOHN 4:9

It was culturally inappropriate for Jesus to ask a Samaritan woman for a drink or to converse with her at all. Her surprise wasn't offense; it was pure curiosity. Jesus defied the norms of his day, and he calls us to do the same. We should not be surprised when Jesus' gracious kindness extends to people, as well as in places, that we are not naturally drawn to.

Yet, even when we are surprised, it can draw us deeper into connection with Jesus through our inquisitiveness. The Samaritan woman was not being obstinate. She asked a question based on the expectations of the culture at the time. We can ask Jesus questions, even—and especially—when he surprises us. He longs to connect with us, and he pursues us in order to get our attention. We don't need to have a perfect reply because that is not what true relationship is about. Let's let down our defenses of perfectionism and engage with Jesus where and as we are.

*Jesus, your love knows no bounds. I love that you didn't interact with only those whom society and religion accepted. You showed us that God's love extends beyond human biases and borders. Thank you.*

## Living Water

Jesus replied, "If you only knew who I am and the gift that God wants to give you, you'd ask me for a drink, and I would give you living water."

JOHN 4:10

Even though Jesus wanted a drink of fresh water from the well, he knew he had something even more satisfying to offer the Samaritan woman. Psalm 78:15–16 recounts how God provided for his people in the past: "In the days of desert dryness, he split open the mighty rock…He gave them all they wanted to drink from his living springs." And Psalm 107:35 talks about what God is able to still do: "He also can turn a barren wilderness into an oasis with water! He can make springs flow into desert lands."

The living water of Christ is available to you. You have only to ask for a drink. His presence is satisfying, and he gives all that you want and need. It doesn't matter how desolate your life appears. He can turn the most barren wilderness into an oasis. Drink your fill and return to him as often as you like. He is more than willing to quench your thirst.

*Giver of Life, though I can offer you a little, what you offer in return is far better. Thank you for the willingness of your heart to pour out your living water of love into my life. I am yours.*

# But How?

The woman replied, "But sir, you don't even have a bucket, and the well is very deep. So where do you find this 'living water'?"

JOHN 4:11

Jesus' offer to the Samaritan woman didn't make sense to her. We don't know the tone of this text. Was she being facetious, or was she genuinely curious? We don't know for certain. However, whatever her attitude, we know this didn't stop the interaction. Many of us have learned to just shrug our shoulders and keep moving on when we don't understand something. We figure we should already know, so we don't press in to actually understand. This is not what the example of Christ shows us, though.

You don't have to be afraid of Jesus misinterpreting your motives. You also don't need to keep yourself from asking him questions. He is relational; he welcomes your curiosity. Even when Jesus' invitations don't make sense to your practical understanding, you can engage with him in further dialogue. You don't have to pretend to know what he is talking about when you don't. Continue to connect with your Savior, for he cares for you.

*Savior, thank you for all that you offer. I am so humbled to know that I can't offend you. I will not hold back my honest reactions and questions from you.*

## Generational Loyalty

> "Do you really think that you are greater than our ancestor Jacob who dug this well and drank from it himself, along with his children and livestock?"
>
> JOHN 4:12

The Samaritan woman may have been being a bit playful in this interaction. She had just finished asking Jesus where his bucket to draw water was, and now she was implying that he would need to dig a new and somehow greater well than Jacob's. Jacob was a common ancestor between the Jews and the Samaritans, and yet these two groups differed on tradition and had few dealings with each other.

Jesus knows our conditioning, that we are brought up to believe certain cultural, familial, and religious traditions. He doesn't condemn us for that. He only has a problem with it when it closes our hearts off in pride, keeping us from being willing to grow in our understanding outside of our limited knowledge. Let's be willing to engage with ideas and traditions outside of our generational loyalties, letting the curiosity of our hearts lead us. Jesus reveals truth to those searching for it. We don't have to be afraid of our honest questions.

*Jesus, I do believe that you are greater than even the wisest of people. I won't let my small understanding keep me from seeing you in the wildness of the world. I believe you will meet me there.*

## *Spring of Life*

Jesus answered, "If you drink from Jacob's well, you'll be thirsty again, but if anyone drinks the living water I give them, they will never be thirsty again. For when you drink the water I give you, it becomes a gushing fountain of the Holy Spirit, flooding you with endless life!"

JOHN 4:13–14

The priests and prophets of this world—even the great ones—can only offer what satisfies for a time. It is not meant to be our sole sustenance. It should point us to Jesus, our great Mediator. In Christ, we can know God for ourselves. We can experience his power in our lives and in our communities. We don't have to wait for a fresh word from a human. He offers us the Holy Spirit, who continually satisfies us from the inside out.

What well have you been drinking from? Perhaps you have found yourself looking to moguls or influencers, drinking up their offerings. How long does that satisfaction last? We were created for reciprocity in our relationships—with the earth, with God, and with each other. If we find ourselves consuming far more than connecting, it is time to redirect ourselves to the true Source of life. In his living waters, we come alive.

*Spirit, thank you for your fountain of life inside of me. Pour into me fresh waters that revive my heart, my hope, and my perspective.*

## Initial Desire

The woman replied, "Let me drink that water so I'll never be thirsty again and won't have to come back here to draw water."

JOHN 4:15

The woman probably had more than one reason to not want to have to come back to the well for water. It would have been convenient, but it also would have kept her from facing her shame day after day. Most of the women came in the morning to draw water together. It was a social activity as much as it was a necessary one. Yet we know that this woman did not feel welcome because of her lifestyle.

Our initial desire for change may come from a place of wanting to escape our pain, shame, or the drudgery of what our lives have become. It is real! Jesus draws us with loving-kindness. This was not the end of his interaction with the woman at the well, and he was not offended by her frank answer. Think of what drew you to Jesus at first. There is no fault in whatever it was, for it was the seed of desire.

*Jesus, you are better than I expected you to be. You meet me in my pain and offer relief from my shame. Thank you.*

## Truth Teller

"But I'm not married," the woman answered. "That's true," Jesus said, "for you've been married five times, and now you're living with a man who is not your husband. You have told the truth."

JOHN 4:17–18

The woman made an honest confession to Jesus, revealing that she had no husband. Jesus, full of surprises, then went on to tell her the truth about her history. He revealed that he already knew her life. Not only this, but he had also already approached her to receive the living water he had to offer. If this doesn't break our boxes of God's goodness, I don't know what will. Jesus demonstrated his saving love to a divorcée from outside of the Jewish faith. She was not, I expect, someone many of us would see as an ideal representative for his message. And yet she was just that!

Think about the last time you were confronted with truth about your life and how that truth affected you. Jesus never shies away from the truth. He does not sugarcoat our failures, and he also does not condemn us for them. He speaks the truth in love always. May we receive it and do the same.

*Savior, you already know me through and through. I won't hide from you today.*

# A Longing to Know More

> The woman changed the subject. "You must be a prophet!
> So tell me this: Why do our fathers worship God on this nearby
> mountain, but your people teach that Jerusalem is the place
> where we must worship. Who is right?"
>
> JOHN 4:19–20

Astounded by Jesus' knowledge of her life, the woman at the well engaged in an intellectual discussion with Jesus. She must have been wondering about this for a while to be so prepared to ask this question. The woman's longing to know which place was the right one to worship God reveals her heart to know the truth.

We should not be afraid to allow the questions of our hearts to bubble to the surface as we connect with Jesus. He may not answer us the way we expect, but he will answer us, nonetheless. He holds the wisdom we long for, and in him is more freedom than we can expect to experience. Just consider the answer Jesus gave in verses 21 through 24. The longing to know more is not presumptive; it is what will drive us further into the revelation of God's heart and his ways.

*Wise God, thank you for never turning away my questions.*
*You do not dissuade them at all, and for that, I am grateful.*
*I give you my whole, curious self today.*

## Engaging the Heart

"Believe me, dear woman, the time has come when you will worship the Father neither on a mountain nor in Jerusalem, but in your heart."

JOHN 4:21

In response to the Samaritan woman's question of where the right place to worship was, Jesus engaged her heart rather than her mind. Worshiping God—surrendering to him and communing with him—is not about the place but rather the posture of our hearts. The old ways of becoming right with God have been put to an end through Jesus, and the new way has come. Through Christ, we are made right, no matter where we are in the world.

We don't have to go searching for sacred spaces or holy ground in order to meet God. He meets us in the realm of our hearts. This is astoundingly good news! Engage the heart of God today even as he engages yours. Right here and now, turn your attention to the nearness of his presence. He is with you, waiting to connect with you. Bow your heart before him and worship him right where you are.

*Lord, thank you for the mystery of knowing you in the deepest spaces of my heart. I welcome you to move in me today as I humble myself before you.*

## Experiential Worship

"Your people don't really know the One they worship, but we Jews worship out of our experience, for it's from the Jews that salvation is available."

JOHN 4:22

The fact that Jesus Christ was born a Jew was no accident. Through him would come salvation for all. Through him, we are able to know who God truly is and to worship him in spirit and in truth. Every human is made in the image of God; that is always true. Jesus came to show us what the Father is truly like, to break down the walls of empty tradition and power structures, and to connect to their Creator every person who comes to him.

Salvation is only possible through Christ, and he was a Jewish man. However, we do not need to become part of the Jewish nation to know him. This is true of any other label as well. We love to align ourselves with identities that divide rather than unite. It doesn't matter what denomination we are a part of if we are surrendered to Christ and worship him. His love welcomes everyone, and the power of his mercy reaches even to the ends of the earth.

*Jesus Christ, thank you for making a way for all to know the power of your liberating love. It is you whom I worship and adore above every affiliation, government, or power structure of this world.*

## *Right Heart*

"From now on, worshiping the Father will not be a matter of the right place but with a right heart. For God is a Spirit, and he longs to have sincere worshipers who adore him in the realm of the Spirit and in truth."

JOHN 4:23–24

Worship God wherever your feet are planted today. Don't put it off until you are in a gathering of believers. Don't even wait until the end of your day. Embrace the Lord's presence in your heart, worshiping him in an overflow of adoration. Welcome his Spirit no matter what it is you are doing at the moment. He longs to be a part of your day, walking with you in the mundane.

We can overspiritualize our experiences in life, thinking that giving God an uninterrupted hour is better than inviting him into moments of connection throughout our day. Not many of us have an hour to give to prayer and Scripture reading. But we all have a few minutes. Those minutes add up. The connection is richer when we remain accessible. Invite the Spirit into your day and let it be an open conversation that runs through it.

*Spirit, I don't want to give you a limited amount of my attention. I welcome you into the whole of my experience, the ups and downs, the joys and the frustrations. Speak to me, and I will do the same to you.*

## The Time Is Now

Jesus said to her, "You don't have to wait any longer,
the Anointed One is here speaking with you—
I am the One you're looking for."

JOHN 4:26

Jesus the Messiah was long awaited not only by the Jewish nation but by every nation. The woman at the well knew that the Anointed One was coming and that he would reveal what they needed to know. Jesus, revealing his true identity, disclosed to this woman what he had only revealed to a few before. He was the one they had been awaiting. What a beautiful gift this was to her—and to us today.

There is no need to wait a moment longer to experience the all-consuming love of Christ. He has more comfort with which to wrap you up than you can imagine. His peace passes all understanding. His joy is deep, like a spring-fed lake that is always receiving fresh water. Consider what you have been waiting for, and let today be the day you let yourself receive the abundance of Christ's kingdom right here and now. He is the perfect portion we are looking for. He has more than enough grace to infuse our lives. Today is all we have. This moment is our invitation to receive what God offers.

*Messiah, unveil the eyes of my heart to see you here and now, right where I am.*

## Surprised by Jesus

At that moment, his disciples returned and were stunned to see Jesus speaking with a Samaritan woman, yet none of them dared ask him why or what they were discussing.

JOHN 4:27

When the disciples saw Jesus conversing with a woman at the well, they were surprised. As we already know, this was a breach of cultural tradition. It is a wonderful revelation of God's heart to know that he cannot be bound by our guidelines of proper etiquette. Though the disciples may have felt shocked and even scandalized at his boldness, Jesus did not back down or explain himself.

When we follow the ways of Jesus, we can expect to be misunderstood by some. We may even offend people around us by not letting rules keep us from showing the compassion of Christ. This is no reason to stop. Christ cares for those we overlook, avoid, and are offended by. If we want to be like him, then it stands to reason that we will surprise people in the process. May we have boldness to love without border, just as Jesus did.

*Compassionate One, it is your example I follow, not the traditions of fearful people. Compel me with your love as I continually yield to your leadership.*

## Spreading the Invitation

All at once, the woman left her water jar and ran off to her village and told everyone, "Come and meet a man at the well who told me everything I've ever done! He could be the One we've been waiting for."

JOHN 4:28–29

Once Jesus revealed his true identity to the woman at the well, she dropped everything and ran back to the village with the news. It was too good to keep to herself! Consider the power of this. She was an outcast in society, drawing water at the hottest part of the day. Yet it was she to whom Jesus revealed himself. She became the message bearer of his goodness that day.

Have you ever received such wonderful news that you dropped everything you were doing to share it? Just as the Samaritan woman proudly shared her experience with others, inviting them to see for themselves, we can do the same. Jesus Christ knows us through and through, and he loves us all the same. This is good news worthy of sharing.

*Anointed One, I am humbled by your love and kindness toward me. As I consider all you have done and all that you offer, I cannot stay silent about your goodness today.*

## Moved to See for Themselves

Hearing this, the people came streaming out of the village
to go see Jesus.

JOHN 4:30

There is power in being known. The Samaritan woman is an example of someone whom God did not overlook. Though society may have shunned her, Jesus welcomed her. Yet it was with this same community that she shared her experience. The woman's act was as gracious as Jesus' engaging with her at the well.

Upon hearing that there was someone who knew the woman's whole life without being told, the curiosity of the people led them to find this man for themselves. They went out to see what it was all about, to see whether this supposed Anointed One was truly the one they had been waiting for. The boldness of the Samaritan woman, as well as her invitation for them to experience for themselves what she had experienced, led a whole village to the well. Let's not underestimate our influence, no matter who we are.

*Jesus, I know that good news is meant to be shared and that our communities thrive when we experience united efforts. Give me boldness to invite others into the experiences I have had so they can benefit themselves.*

## Satisfying Purpose

Jesus told them, "I have eaten a meal you don't know about."...
To clarify, Jesus spoke up and said, "My food is to do the will of
him who sent me and bring it to completion."

JOHN 4:32, 34

The disciples had left Jesus at the well to go buy food in the village. When they returned, they walked in on an interaction that astounded them. As they offered Jesus the food that they had brought back, he told them that he didn't need to eat. He had been filled by a much greater purpose while they were away.

Jesus' needs were satisfied by doing the will of God. In his interaction and invitation with the woman at the well, his satisfaction was in her glad reception. Not only this, but she also went and brought back with her a whole village for him to minister the loving truth of God. The satisfaction he felt in his soul—the purpose and manifestation of his ministry—was better than any he could find in eating at that moment.

*Jesus, I have known soul satisfaction that takes my mind off my natural needs, just as you did. Fulfilling a wonderful purpose brings so much satisfaction. Refresh my vision so that I may walk in yours today.*

# Ripe and Ready

As the crowds emerged from the village, Jesus said to his disciples, "Why would you say, 'The harvest is another four months away'? Look at all the people coming—now is harvest time! Their hearts are like vast fields of ripened grain—ready for a harvest."

JOHN 4:35

Jesus often taught in parables and word pictures. These were easy things for the people to understand if they could only perceive the power of the comparison. When Jesus described the crowds as a ripe harvest, the hearers knew that the time was right for a spiritual harvest.

Even if we are not familiar with farming, many of us can still imagine lush fields of wheat or corn, ripe and ready for the picking. Even when the natural cycle of seasons is a ways off, the spiritual season we are in may be full of life. We may find ourselves in the cold, barren months of winter all while experiencing a spiritual summer, full of spiritual abundance. We must be aware of the season we are in so that we can do what is ours to do as we partner with the Keeper of the Harvest.

*Lord, give me eyes to see and a heart of understanding and discernment to know what spiritual season I am in.*

## Rewards of Reaping

> "Everyone who reaps these souls for eternal life will receive a reward. Both those who plant spiritual seeds and those who reap the spiritual harvest will celebrate together with great joy!"
>
> JOHN 4:36

Many in this world do not know the incredible love of the Father. Jesus described these people who had yet to discover his goodness as being a part of a "great harvest." The statement of Jesus in John 4:36 encourages us to share his wonderful life, his glorious light, and his expansive love with those around us.

Perhaps you can think of people in your life whose souls are ready to receive the incomparable love of God. Jesus promises that those who reap these souls will receive a reward. There is incredible joy and celebration in both planting the seeds and reaping the harvest. This is not something done forcefully. It is always an invitation, without guilt or manipulation. There is liberty for all of us in the great kingdom of our God.

*Lord, open my eyes to see whom I can share your wonderful love with today, no strings attached. I know that your truth always draws people in with kindness and clarity.*

## Some Sow, Some Harvest

"I have sent you out to harvest a field that you haven't planted, where many others have labored long and hard before you. And now you are privileged to profit from their labors and reap the harvest."

JOHN 4:38

We should not be discouraged when we have played a part in sowing the seeds of God's love into a person's life. The tilling of soil and planting of seeds are as necessary to the harvest as going out and reaping the fruit of it. It is wise to recognize where others are now so that we don't try to force them into a decision that they are not prepared to make. We can trust God with the timing; we do what is ours to do in the season we are in.

Just as there is no hierarchy in God's kingdom, no part of the process of a person's spiritual development is better or worse than another. We have the privilege of partnering with God in meeting people where they are. We don't have to force a thing. In the same way, our own lives follow the rhythm of the cycles of the natural world. There is no need to fight where we are, for Christ meets us in the midst of our reality.

*Great Harvester, I partner with your ways, following your leading and incorporating your wisdom into my life. I do the work that is here and now, knowing it will prepare the way for what is to come.*

March

## Power of One Testimony

Many from the Samaritan village became believers in Jesus
because of the woman's testimony:
"He told me everything I ever did!"

JOHN 4:39

Your testimony holds tremendous power. The willingness of one person to share her story completely changed a village. Many more came to believe in Jesus as the Savior of the world because of the Samaritan woman's boldness. Don't be afraid to share your own breakthroughs with others, for it may just be the spark that ignites someone else's heart.

The woman at the well didn't have to go back to her village and share her experience with everyone. But her willingness to do so was an invitation for others to experience the same. Consider those with whom you could share the testimony of goodness in your life and invite them to experience the same. Our breakthroughs pave the way for the breakthroughs of others. Healing and freedom are meant to be as communal as they are personal.

*Savior, thank you for what you have done in my life. When you move in mighty ways, I will not keep the news to myself. Thank you for your power that reaches beyond my little life to bring hope and encouragement to others.*

## Gracious Jesus

Then they begged Jesus to stay with them,
so he stayed there for two days,
resulting in many more coming to faith in him
because of his message.

JOHN 4:40–41

Jesus answers the cries of those who hunger and thirst for righteousness. The Samaritan village surely wanted Jesus to stay more than two days, but he had more places to go. He did not just rush away from them, however. He spent time with them, feeding them with the nourishment of the Father's loving truth.

Jesus is so gracious with us. It is also so important to recognize that though Jesus could not give them the rest of his days, he offered them what he could. We must do the same. We each have limited resources to offer, and clear boundaries around them allow us to give what we can without feeling resentful. Being gracious does not mean setting aside our priorities to please others. We can meet people where they are and still remain rooted in our purpose.

*Gracious One, how you love ministering to the hungry and satisfying their needs with the nourishment of your loving truth. I want to be gracious and rooted in my life, just as you were in your ministry. Help me to grow in grounded purpose and to be liberal with grace.*

## Personal Faith

> The Samaritans said to the woman, "Now we've heard him
> ourselves. We no longer believe just because of what you told us,
> but we're convinced that he really is the true Savior of the world!"
>
> JOHN 4:42

It may have been the Samaritan woman's testimony and invitation that drew the village to go see Jesus for themselves, but it was their own experiences with Jesus that made their faith personal. Perhaps we have been going to church our whole lives, following the traditions and expectations of our parents. Maybe we have heard about how good Jesus is—the sweetness and freedom of his love. Until we experience it for ourselves, we may remain unconvinced of the power of God.

It is not a bad thing to want more out of our spiritual experiences than what we have yet known. Curiosity may draw us to get to know Jesus, but once we come face-to-face with his loving-kindness, feed on his wisdom, and truly see him for who he is, we can then come into our own personal faith. Jesus said, "How enriched you are when you crave righteousness!" (Matthew 5:6). He will satisfy you with the fruitfulness of his kingdom.

*Savior, knowing you—not just knowing about you—is such a great gift. Deepen my faith as I press into your presence. I want to know you more, Lord.*

# The Hometown Conundrum

Jesus knew that prophets are honored everywhere
except in their own hometown.

JOHN 4:44

Why is it that the people who knew us best when we were growing up cannot imagine that we could be anything but who we were then? Even Jesus experienced this disbelief in his potential when he was in Galilee. He had been traveling and performing miracles, teaching the wisdom of God, and healing the sick. Yet, in his hometown, he knew he would encounter those who would not believe he was the Son of God.

Think about a time when you encountered someone from a different time in your life and what that experience was like. Now think of a time when you came across a long-lost friend, schoolmate, or relative. Did you expect them to remain unchanged? We all grow—not only physically but also emotionally, socially, and cognitively. We are allowed to change our minds about things as we mature. Let's allow ourselves, as well as those in our lives, the room to transform and offer each other support for where we are now.

*Messiah, even you came up against skepticism in your life. Not everyone who knew you actually saw you for who you were. That is a comfort to me now. I will not neglect or deny who I am becoming just because someone else can't validate it.*

## Undeterred

Jesus said to him, "You never believe unless you see signs and wonders." But the man continued to plead, "Come with me to Capernaum before my little boy dies!" Jesus looked him in the eyes and said, "Go back home now. I promise you, your son will live." The man believed in his heart the words of Jesus and set off for home.

JOHN 4:48–50

Jesus never turns away a persistent heart. This should give us courage to keep coming to him, to keep pressing in with prayer, and to keep our hearts open to his voice. Jesus was in the town where he had turned water into wine, and the man who approached him knew that Jesus could miraculously heal his son.

The man left Jesus' presence believing that what Jesus said was true, and he was met with good news on his way. We should never be afraid to be bold before Jesus. We also need to take his words to heart. As we get to know the nature of Christ, we can rest in the faithfulness that trusting him brings.

*Christ, thank you for receiving me as I am. I know I don't have to hide my cares from you. Thank you for the power of your love. I will be bold before you, knowing you are gracious with me.*

# The Exact Moment

The father immediately realized that it was at that very same hour that Jesus spoke the words to him, "Your son will live." From that day forward, the man, his servants, and all his family believed.

JOHN 4:53

When Jesus speaks life, breakthrough comes at that very moment. We can count on Jesus' help when we need it. As we persistently look to him for answers to our greatest problems, he speaks words of life over us. When he does, he releases breakthrough into our lives.

God's power is not limited to what we consider the best conditions. He meets us in the impossibility of our circumstances, and he can turn our mourning into dancing. When we seek him out, doing what he says to do in response to our pleas, we will not only find peace. We will also experience overwhelming joy as we realize his incomparable goodness. There is no better time to trust him. Today is the day of our present peace and joyful expectation.

*Wonderful One, when you speak, heaven and earth move in response. There is nothing you cannot do. I believe this to be true. I will not wallow in despair today. I dare to hope in your all-consuming love.*

# *Pools of Kindness*

Inside the city, near the Sheep Gate, there is a pool called in
Aramaic, The House of Loving Kindness, surrounded by five
covered porches.

JOHN 5:2

In the temple of the Lord in Jerusalem, there was a pool of
healing waters called *Beit-Hesed*, or Bethesda, meaning
"House of Loving Kindness." Here, those needing physical
healing would wait for an angel to come and stir the waters.
The first to step into the waters "after the waters swirled
would instantly be healed" (John 5:4).

Even under the Old Covenant, there was hope for healing. In Christ, no one is left out of his powerful kindness.
There is no competition to see who can reach him first, for
he welcomes all with the same wonderful love, no matter
how long it takes them to approach. He is full of healing for
all who come to him. His presence has become our House
of Loving Kindness, and there is no need to wait a moment
longer to jump into the healing waters that his Spirit stirs
within us.

*Kind God, thank you for the power of your love that never
diminishes or wears out. I come fully aware of the realities of
my limitations, awaiting the power of your Spirit to fill me
with the refreshingly healing waters of your kindness.*

# Waiting for Their Healing

Hundreds of sick people were lying under the covered porches—
the paralyzed, the blind, and the crippled—
all of them waiting for their healing.

JOHN 5:3

We live in a world full of heartache. Everyone we meet has some sort of challenge they are facing. While many may be able to hide their challenges, still others of us cannot. But remember that we are all the beloved of God no matter what we look like, where we come from, or what we can or cannot do. Those who are paralyzed, are blind, or have other physical disabilities are not second-class citizens. God loves them wholly, just as they are, the same as he loves any other. In the kingdom of Christ, all are brothers and sisters, beloved children of the Most High.

If we have lived long enough, we know the struggle of waiting. In a society that promotes instant gratification, when we do have to wait, it can be frustrating. In life, however, some of the best things are those that take a while to develop or come to us. May we learn to embrace the waiting seasons, for there is purpose in the most mundane aspects of our lives if we are willing to recognize them for their beauty.

*Jesus, I will not wish away today by overvaluing what is to come. Your grace is sufficient, it is beautiful, and it is mine now.*

## Permission to Heal

Among the many sick people lying there was a man who had been disabled for thirty-eight years. When Jesus saw him lying there, he knew that the man had been crippled for a long time. Jesus said to him, "Do you truly long to be well?"

JOHN 5:5–6

Even though Jesus knew the history of the man with disabilities, he did not make any assumptions about his desires. God, in the same way, does not force us to receive anything from him. He is a God of consent. He cares for us enough to give us a choice in the matter. Again, Jesus knew this man's history, and it is probable that Jesus also knew his heart. Even so, his question to the man was an invitation to agency.

If we want to emulate Christ's life, then we must look at his interactions with others. He did not force himself on others. He engaged them in conversation and asked them questions to probe their hearts. This is a powerful model to follow. We cannot force our faith on anyone else, for that is not the way of Christ. He does not manipulate or make assumptions. He invites others to engage with him. This, too, is a reflection of his goodness.

*Loving Lord, thank you for inviting us into a relationship with you. You don't simply tell us what to do. You welcome our perspectives, our personalities, and our choice. What a wonderful God you are!*

## Different Expectations

The sick man answered, "Sir, there's no way I can get healed, for I have no one to lower me into the water when the angel comes. As soon as I try to crawl to the edge of the pool, someone else jumps in ahead of me."

JOHN 5:7

This man had been waiting a long time for his healing. He had stayed at this pool long enough to see the waters stirred multiple times, failing to reach it before another jumped in. In this circumstance, it seemed to be every man for himself, rushing so that they would not miss out on their healing. This is not the way of the kingdom, however.

Jesus saw this man and all of his longing. Jesus asked him whether he truly longed to be healed, and in the man's answer, Jesus could clearly see that he did. Jesus sees your heart as well. He knows the expectations of your heart, the way you feel defeated in certain areas of your life. When he asks you if you truly want breakthrough, your answer reveals your heart. No matter your expectations, his love is powerful enough to break through your disappointment and liberate you in grander ways than you can imagine.

*Healer, even in my disappointing past, you see through my self-protection, past my defenses to the heart of my desire. Thank you for seeing me as I am.*

# No Need to Earn a Thing

> Jesus said to him, "Stand up! Pick up your sleeping mat and you will walk!" Immediately he stood up—he was healed! So he rolled up his mat and walked again! Now Jesus worked this miracle on the Sabbath.
>
> JOHN 5:8–9

What a wonderfully gracious healer Jesus is. This man had to do no more than to express his desire to be healed, however hidden in his disappointment from his past, in order to receive the power of Jesus' healing in his body. Though Jesus' interactions with those he healed varied from person to person, the result was the same: incredible liberation.

We do not need to earn our healing. As recipients of God's love, we don't strive for the gift he willingly offers. Have you been trying to earn your place in someone's life? Perhaps you have felt like you need to become a better version of yourself before you are worthy of love. Come to Christ just as you are today. You don't have to earn a thing in order to receive his wonderful kindness. He is good, he is generous, and he is with you.

*Lord Jesus, thank you for the wonderful gift of your love. Thank you for the power of your presence that offers more freedom than I could hope for. I am yours.*

## *Naysayers*

> When the Jewish leaders saw the man walking along carrying his sleeping mat, they objected and said, "What are you doing carrying that? Don't you know it's the Sabbath? It's not lawful for you to carry things on the Sabbath!"
>
> JOHN 5:10

After a dramatic encounter with Jesus, the healed man was going on his merry way, doing exactly what Jesus had told him to do. As the man walked on his way, Jewish leaders saw him and chastised him for carrying his mat on the Sabbath. Jewish tradition didn't allow any work—including carrying a mat—on the Sabbath.

Have we ever criticized someone for doing what the Lord had told them to because it didn't fit with our traditions or rules? Jesus brings liberation not only from sin but also from the confines of religious conditioning. If we walk in obedience to God's leading in our lives, we are free from the limits of others. This does not mean, however, that we can escape the criticism of others. It will always be there. Let's determine to follow the expansive ways of Christ, which put the value of relational love over the letter of the law. God's ways can offend those who do not know his heart, but that is no reason to abandon his ways in order to fit in with others.

*Jesus, I trust that your ways are better than the limitations of religion.*

# Walk Away from Sin

A short time later, Jesus found the man at the temple and said to him, "Look at you now! You're healed! Walk away from your sin so that nothing worse will happen to you."

JOHN 5:14

Jesus willingly meets us where we are, offering us his love that washes away our shame, fear, and doubt. He stands willing to intervene in our lives. Once he moves on our behalf, he does make a request of us. It is the same thing he said to the man he had just healed at Bethesda: "Walk away from your sin so that nothing worse will happen to you."

Sin entangles us in cycles of self-destruction. It can erode our lives, destroy families, and even affect our communities. Jesus forgives us of our sins and heals us. What does this inspire within us to change in our lives? There may be behaviors or attitudes that we still need to transform into the perspective of Christ. Let's not be afraid to look openly at what needs to change. Today is the day to make a plan and walk away from everything that hinders love in our lives.

*Lord, help me to face, without a defensive heart, the areas of my life that need change. Lead me with your kindness into how I can more freely walk in your love.*

# Jesus the Healer

The man went to the Jewish leaders to inform them,
"It was Jesus who healed me!"

JOHN 5:15

The Jewish leaders had already asked this man who had healed him. At the time of their query, the man did not even know who Jesus was. When he had another encounter with Christ, Jesus' identity became clear to the man. Going back to the Jewish leaders, the man revealed Jesus' identity. The news was still good. He was healed, and healing had come through Jesus from Nazareth.

We cannot control how people will react to the good news of the gospel. We cannot know what they will do with that information. Even so, it is not a reason to keep quiet. When we have encountered freedom and healing from the Lord, it is wonderful news to share. How has he transformed your life with his kindness? Share it with someone today.

*Healer, you do so much more than extend grace. You flood my life with your tangible acts of mercy. Your kindness is unmatched. Move in me, and I will tell of your goodness. Reveal your power through my life, flowing into the lives of others. Transform individuals, families, and communities through your wonderful love.*

# Offense Clouds the Heart

From that day forward the Jewish leaders began
to persecute Jesus because of the things he did
on the Sabbath.

JOHN 5:16

E ven though everything Jesus did was what the Father
did, the religious leaders, who should have known the
character of God, chose to persecute Jesus rather than honor
him. They could not see the truth of who he was because of
the offense in their hearts. They could not see past their own
interpretation of what mattered to God in order to hear the
invitation to greater freedom in the love of God.

Offense builds walls, whereas love breaks them down.
When we sense ourselves shutting off from hearing others'
points of view, we may be letting pride build a wall between
us and them. This is never the way of God. This is not the
way of Christ. He leads us beyond our understanding,
inviting us to follow him on the humble path of his mercy.
We cannot presume to know more than he does. We must
humble our hearts; this will help us to remain open in
compassion rather than shut down by an unwillingness to
recognize a differing perspective.

*Lord, I don't want to persecute anyone because of my own
offense. Your love is larger than earthly systems, and I will
prioritize you even when my understanding is incomplete.*

# Never Stops Working

Jesus answered his critics by saying,
"Every day my Father is at work, and I will be, too!"

JOHN 5:17

God never stops moving in marvelous mercy. He is always at work, weaving threads of his love through our lives, creating an intricate tapestry of his kindness. We are each a small part of a larger whole. May we never forget that. Our lives are not at the center of God's plan, and yet each of us is sewn in. We all play a part.

The fact that Jesus healed on the Sabbath is wonderful news for everyone. It means that God has no need to take a break from his goodness. He never stops working. That means that he is up to something good even when we cannot recognize it quite yet. What a wonderful God! What a reason to rejoice and to never lose hope! He has not given up on us, and he is not finished working his miraculous love in our lives. This perspective can shift our thinking just enough so that we dare to hope rather than to sink into despair. Jesus Christ is good, and he will never stop working.

*Father, thank you for relentlessly moving in mercy in this world. I trust that you aren't finished yet and that there is reason yet to hope.*

## Together with the Father

Jesus said, "I speak to you eternal truth. The Son is unable to do anything from himself or through his own initiative. I only do the works that I see the Father doing, for the Son does the same works as his Father."

JOHN 5:19

This "eternal truth" that Jesus spoke of is significant in many ways. It means that before he was born into a human body, Christ was doing the works of the Father. It also signifies that he will never stop moving on the Father's behalf. That means that today—right at this very moment—when Christ moves in our lives, he is doing what he sees the Father doing.

The Father, Son, and Spirit move in complete unity with one another. They are inextricably linked, and they do nothing with their own motives in mind. They are one. They are one in purpose. When we look to the ministry of Christ, we catch a glimpse of the beautifully humble heart of the Father. He is full of love, of power, and of generous grace. He reaches out to the weak ones, welcoming in those the world casts out. He is good. He is patient. He is unflinching in his identity. He is glorious and yet oh so approachable.

*God, thank you. I love you.*

## Loving Revelation

"Because the Father loves his Son so much, he always reveals to him everything that he is about to do. And you will all be amazed when he shows him even greater works than what you've seen so far!"

JOHN 5:20

Revelation comes from a longing of love to share goodness with others. Whenever you experience a deeper understanding of God's mercy through the Spirit's fellowship within you, it is a gift of love. When you catch a glimpse of expansiveness of God's kindness, it is out of a place of connection with the love of God. Everything God reveals about who he is and what he does is from a place of love toward us. How incredible is that?

Practice this same attitude today as you share with your loved ones something about yourself. Being open with them can be an act of love toward them. Just like God invites us to participate in his plans, invite your loved ones to join you in something you are about to do, and they may feel encouraged to participate. Widen your net today, welcoming those closest to you to be a part of what you are planning.

*Good God, thank you for the example you set in inclusive planning. Rather than standing on the outside, you invite us in to partner with your heart. Help me do the same with others.*

## Life-Giving Power

"For just as the Father has power to raise the dead, the Son will also raise the dead and give life to whomever he wants."

JOHN 5:21

Just as Jesus walked in the authority of his Father, we also walk in the authority that Jesus offers to us. Jesus moves in life, building people up, taking their burdens, and freeing them from their bondage. Whatever we do in his name, we must also do in the same spirit. We are called to be kind to others, to build each other up in authentic love, and to relieve the burdens of those who are weighed down by the cruelties of life.

We cannot claim to be like Jesus if we are not walking in the ways of his laid-down love. We must follow his path of humble mercy, never turning away a hungry heart. We cannot chase the attention of the powerful, longing for their approval. We must stand strong in the compassion of Christ, no matter what. This means laying down judgment, classism, elitism, and our personal preferences. We pick up the tools of generosity, patience, peacemaking, and outrageous kind-heartedness in their place.

*Life-Giver, where I have aligned with destructive forces, I repent. Renew my mind and heart in your powerful mercy. I choose to follow your ways.*

## Honor Begets Honor

"The Father judges no one, for he has given to the Son all the authority to judge. Therefore, the honor that belongs to the Father he will now share with his Son. So if you refuse to honor the Son, you are refusing to honor the Father who sent him."

JOHN 5:22–23

Jesus holds all power to judge and to forgive. The Father shared this authority with the Son, trusting him to represent his heart accurately. When we honor Jesus Christ as the Son of God, giving him our worship and devotion, we, in extension, also offer the Father that same honor. As a representative of the Father, Jesus revealed the priorities of God's kingdom to all who were open to hear.

As believers in Christ, we have also become representatives of his kingdom. How accurately are we demonstrating the heart of the Father in our lives? This is a fair question to ask. There is so much grace in the fellowship we have with Jesus, but the first place to start is with an honest look at our intentions, our priorities, and our practices. May we honor Christ with how we live our lives, for he is worthy.

*Jesus Christ, you are worthy of my submission and my honor. I want to represent you well, reflecting your gracious generosity through my choices.*

## Come Alive in Christ

"I speak to you an eternal truth: if you embrace my message and believe in the One who sent me, you will never face condemnation. In me, you have already passed from the realm of death into eternal life!"

JOHN 5:24

Jesus offers us grounded goodness in this life, but he also offers us a hope that goes beyond, to the realm of eternal life. Time in these mortal bodies is limited, but that does not mean death is the end of life, just life as we know it. Believing in Christ has so many benefits. Trusting his ability and desire to save and heal us leads us to the liberating love of the Father. What a glorious reality!

If we truly embrace the message of Christ in our lives, we come alive in the kingdom of his everlasting goodness. There we will experience the expanse of his kindness forever. His light will never dim, and our hopes will all be filled. "He will wipe away every tear from their eyes and eliminate death entirely. No one will mourn or weep any longer. The pain of wounds will no longer exist, for the old order has ceased" (Revelation 21:4). What an anticipated day that is!

*God, thank you for the hope I have in you. You are my greatest confidence.*

# Authority from the Father

"As the Father is the source of life, so he has given the Son the power to impart life. The Father has transferred to the Son the authority to judge, because he is the Son of Man."

JOHN 5:26–27

Christ has the power to impart life. We know that he raised the dead in his ministry on the earth. He also breathes hope into barren hearts. He welcomes the lonely, encourages the downhearted, and heals the sick. All that he did and does is with life-giving power. This all comes from the power of his love. It is a part of all that he does, for love is who God is (see 1 John 4:16).

The authority of the Father is Christ's. Whatever Christ offers us, therefore, is an extension of the Father. Luke 9:1 says that "Jesus summoned together his twelve apostles and imparted to them authority over every demon and the power to heal every disease." Jesus did not keep to himself the authority the Father had given him. He shared it with his closest friends and trusted companions. We cannot hoard our influence and think that we are being Christlike. Even our influence and power are things that God means for us to share with and offer to trusted people.

*Perfect One, I will not hold on to my position with a tight grip. Instead, teach me how to invite others to walk in shared authority.*

## Not on My Own

"Nothing I do is from my own initiative. As I hear the judgment passed by my Father, I execute those judgments. And my judgments will be perfect, because I seek only to fulfill the desires of my Father who sent me."

JOHN 5:30

If we know that God's perspective is perfect, that he sees everything precisely as it is without filter or pretense, then we can trust that his judgments are just. Not only does he see every reality and possibility, but he is also faithful, just, merciful, and true. He cannot lie, and he does not have any ulterior motives.

Jesus did what the Father revealed to him to do. He relied on his revelation and wisdom to inform his decisions. He knew the Father's heart because he had a deep relationship with him. Jesus was fully God, yes, but he was also fully human. He had to choose to follow his Father's ways just as we get to choose to follow the example of Jesus. Our job is not to judge others but to be obedient to God. It is important that we develop a deep fellowship with the Spirit who reveals the heart of God as we follow Christ.

*Spirit, nothing that I do is on my own. I trust you more than I trust myself. Speak to me, bring me deeper understanding, and lead me. I will follow.*

## No Need for Validation

"I have no need to be validated by men,
but I'm explaining these things so that you
will believe and be saved."

JOHN 5:34

Jesus did not need the validation of others to prove his identity. He already knew who he was. We can learn a lot from this. If we are constantly searching for validation from outside sources, we will shape-shift in order to find approval. We were never meant to find our worth in others' opinions of us. Belonging is a deep need, and we can find it in communities that are safe and supportive. Our worth, however, is intrinsic. It never changes.

How much the opinions of others can sway us will reflect how connected we are to our identities in Christ. We were each created in the image of a loving and good God. We don't need to change a bit in order to be loved. We are loved just as we are at this moment. It is from this place of deep acceptance and belonging that we can transform, bloom, and be free to be who God created us to be.

*Creator, thank you for making me in your image. I am a loving reflection of a kind God. May my roots go deep in your goodness, flooding my sense of self with who you say I am.*

# Supernatural Proof

"I can provide more substantial proof of who I am that
exceeds John's testimony—my miracles! These works
which the Father destined for me to complete—
they prove that the Father has sent me!"

JOHN 5:36

John the Baptizer "was a blazing…torch" that the people
basked in for a short time "with great joy" (v. 35). He was
the forerunner who prepared the way of Jesus, the Messiah.
Jesus later refers to himself as the Light of the World. "Those
who embrace me," he said, "will experience life-giving light,
and…will never walk in darkness" (8:12).

John's light may have burned bright and hot for a short
time, but Jesus' light would never dwindle. This is still true.
Jesus walked in the power of the Spirit, performing many
miracles that spoke of his true identity as God's Son. Have
you ever seen or experienced an inexplicable wonder? The
Spirit of God still moves in supernatural ways through his
people today. It is not out of the question for you to encounter the power of God in mysterious ways. Ask, seek, and
knock today. And, more than anything, walk in the light of
his persistent presence.

*Light of the World, you are the one I look to in hard times and
in joyous ones. Move with mighty power in my life and in this
world. You are my hope.*

## *Giver of Life*

> "You are busy analyzing the Scriptures, poring over them hoping to gain eternal life. Everything you read points to me, yet you still refuse to come to me so I can give you the life you're looking for—eternal life!"
>
> JOHN 5:39–40

Being devoutly religious does not mean that a person actually knows God. One can know about him and yet totally miss him. This was true when Jesus was ministering on the earth, and it is true today. There were many religious leaders and scholars of the Torah who scoured the texts, believing that if they abided by the letter of the law, they would find eternal life.

However, when the one who led Moses and the Israelites out of their captivity and provided for them in the desert came to them, they did not recognize him. Jesus Christ was sent to lead all who would follow him to the presence of the Father. He came to set the sinner free and to lift the burden of the law by giving us grace. May we not be so concerned with our black-and-white expectations that we miss the goodness of God that is already right here with us.

*Messiah, I don't want to miss you or what you are doing. I yield my life to you, the Living God, and I choose to follow you even when it goes against my religious traditions or conditioning.*

# What Are You Living For?

"I have come to represent my Father, yet you refuse to embrace me in faith. If someone comes in their own name and with their own agenda, you readily accept him. Of course you're unable to believe in me. For you live to enjoy the praises of others and not the praise that comes from the one true God."

JOHN 5:43–44

Powerfully persuasive people can convince others to prioritize what they do, all while serving a purpose that satisfies their own agenda. When we live for the praises of others, we get caught up in performing for them. However, we are set free in Christ to stop performing and to exist as ourselves. Jesus offers love that covers our wrongs, grace that empowers us to stand strong, and mercy that liberates us from our pasts.

Jesus is worth following even when it means sacrificing vain ambitions. He offers discernment to help us see through the empty words and promises of powerful people. He gives wisdom so we can follow his path of love, offering compassion to those we come across. He holds the keys to eternal life and to the abundance of God's kingdom. When we live for his honor and approval, we find soul satisfaction. He is pure in motive, liberal in love, and always trustworthy.

*Jesus, I live for you, for your opinion of me is more important than the shifting ideals of others.*

# More than Ideology

"If you really believed what Moses has written, then you would embrace me, for Moses wrote about me! But since you do not believe what he wrote, no wonder you don't believe what I say."

JOHN 5:46–47

It is not enough for us to value the words of people we respect. Perhaps we quote them reverently, yet we fail to see the scope of their larger mission. Maybe we categorize them in a way that seems all neat and perfect, yet we dismiss the more complicated parts of their humanity. People are not one-dimensional beings. We're not two-dimensional either. Life has so many nuances, so many tensions that remain held in balance with one another.

This is an opportunity to learn from the mistakes of the religious leaders who did not recognize the Messiah before them even though one of their most respected leaders, Moses, wrote of his coming. We cannot dismiss the mysterious ways of God, answering prayers in ways we do not expect. His ways are higher than our ways. We must not confine the power of God to our limited beliefs. We must allow him room and look for the fruit of the Spirit as our guide.

*Jesus, I'm so glad that you are not just an idea. You are living, active, and moving in mercy. Open my eyes to see where you are today.*

## Drawn In

A massive crowd of people followed him everywhere.
They were attracted by his miracles and the healings
they watched him perform.

JOHN 6:2

The signs and wonders of Jesus' ministry attracted massive crowds. They followed him wherever he went. Miracles may have drawn many to him, but Jesus knew that signs would not make everyone believe. The way of faith would require both trust and sacrifice, and not everyone was willing to implement these.

Think of what drew you to Jesus at first. What was it that attracted you to him? Perhaps you were curious about his love, or maybe you simply wanted to find a place of belonging in community. Whatever your story is, remember the beginning. Now think about how your journey of faith has unfolded. What trials have you walked through? What do you believe now that you couldn't have imagined at first? Wherever you find yourself today, Jesus is as accessible to you now as he was then. He is near. Can you sense him drawing you in again?

*Jesus, you are so full of loving-kindness. Wrap me up in your embrace and love me to life in your presence once again.*

# Stretch Your Faith

As Jesus sat down, he looked out and saw the massive crowd of people scrambling up the hill, for they wanted to be near him. So he turned to Philip and said, "Where will we buy enough food to feed all these people?" Now Jesus already knew what he was about to do, but he said this to stretch Philip's faith.

JOHN 6:5–6

God is not only concerned with our spiritual health; he also cares about meeting our physical needs. For every need we have, there is a corresponding way to meet that need on the earth. God designed it this way. He is a faithful provider.

Jesus already knew what he was going to do before he asked Philip how they should feed the crowd of thousands. This was an exercise of stretching Philip's faith, which also meant enlarging his imagination. When was the last time you looked at an impossible circumstance and had to think outside of the box? The good news is that even the stretching of your faith is not the limit of God's powerful ability to provide. Philip's faith was stretched to snack level, but Jesus would provide a satisfying meal. What an encouragement this is!

*Provider, thank you for going above and beyond my small expectations. You are wonderful!*

## Significance of a Little

Just then, Andrew, Peter's brother, spoke up and said, "Look! Here's a young person with five barley loaves and two small fish… but how far would that go with this huge crowd?"

JOHN 6:8–9

It is truly humbling to think of five loaves of bread and two small fish feeding more than a few people. However, in the hands of God, any small offering can multiply its effectiveness. When we look at what we have to offer and see scraps in comparison to the need that is out there, we can choose to see with eyes of expectation. We may not be able to tell how the need will be met, but a little can go a long way in the kindness of God.

Whatever you have been hesitating to either offer or do because of its seeming insignificance in the big picture, choose to offer it to the Lord today. What is his response? If he blesses it, you can be assured that it will not be wasted.

*Jesus, I offer you what little I have and ask you to do something wonderful with it. Show me how I should move ahead, and I will follow your directions. Thank you.*

April

# Miraculous Multiplication

On the vast grassy slope, more than five thousand hungry people sat down. Jesus then took the barley loaves and the fish and gave thanks to God. He then gave it to the disciples to distribute to the people. Miraculously, the food multiplied, with everyone eating as much as they wanted!

JOHN 6:10–11

As the disciples took the loaves and fish around to the people, the food miraculously multiplied. The baskets never emptied. Five thousand men were present, not counting the women and children in attendance. What an astounding miracle this was to everyone who was there!

Remember this when Jesus sends you out with what seems to be too little to make a noticeable change. The God who provided food for the five thousand by blessing the lunch of a young boy is the same God who blesses and multiplies what you offer him. You don't have to wait another moment to share what he has given you. Your offering coupled with his power can do greater things than you can yet anticipate.

*Lord, take my meager offerings and bless them. What I have doesn't seem like much, but it is yours, nonetheless. Provide for others through what little I have to offer.*

# More than Enough

When everyone was satisfied, Jesus told his disciples,
"Now go back and gather up the pieces left over
so that nothing will be wasted."

JOHN 6:12

Even after thousands of people had been fed, many pieces were leftover. The disciples followed Jesus' advice and gathered what was left so that nothing would be wasted. Everyone had eaten until they were satisfied, and still there was a large enough amount to clean up. This is perhaps as astounding as the multiplication of the food in the first place.

What God offers is abundant. He does not give us the bare minimum to get us through. He is extravagantly generous with us. When we are tempted to withhold our own help from others for fear of scarcity, we must remember the open-handedness of God. We partner with the heart of God when we offer what we have without expecting anything in return. Choosing to be generous is choosing to reflect the liberality of God's love. He will surely provide for everyone, and we get to partner with him in meeting others' needs. In the end, there will always be enough for us, too, to eat our fill.

*Provider, thank you for the power of your generosity that doesn't overlook a single person. Soften my heart in your compassion and move me in your mercy.*

## Plentiful Provision

The disciples filled up twelve baskets of fragments,
a basket of leftovers for each disciple.

JOHN 6:13

We can trust God to provide for us when we follow him. The disciples had been part of the miracle, but God did not leave them out of receiving from it either. There were enough leftovers for each of the disciples to have his own basket of food.

Though leftovers may not appeal to the well-fed, the hungry are happy to have food, no matter how it comes. Let's keep ourselves from turning our noses up at what God offers us. It may even be that we find the abundance of what is already in our own hands, within our grasp, to meet our needs. It is important to look for creative solutions and to listen to the voice of the Lord guiding us in his wisdom. He always knows just what to do.

*God of Abundance, open my understanding to see where you are leading me and the steps to take to get there. I trust that you will provide plentifully for my needs, even if the outcome looks different from what I expect. You are so good, God.*

## *Convinced*

All the people were astounded as they saw with their own eyes the incredible miracle Jesus had performed! They began to say among themselves, "He really is the One—the true prophet we've been expecting!"

JOHN 6:14

Seeing with their own eyes what Jesus had done, the people could not explain away the miracle. They began to really believe that he could be the Messiah who was long awaited. Perhaps you have had a similar experience with the Lord moving in a big and mysterious way. Though people who were not with you may have explanations for what it could have been, you cannot be talked out of what you saw with your own eyes.

On the other hand, perhaps you have only heard the whispers of what Jesus can do. In either case, your curiosity and conviction can draw you toward God. If you have yet to experience the transformative power of God's mercy-kindness in your life, press in to know him more. He is not far away! If you have seen him move with your own eyes, let your conviction lead you further to Christ's character. He is good, he is near, and he is for you.

*Lord, you are the God of miracles, and I can't deny it. Thank you for the ways you reveal your kindness through the power of your Spirit. Move again, Lord.*

## Different Desires

*Jesus, knowing that they were about to take him and make him their king by force, quickly left and went up the mountainside alone.*

JOHN 6:15

Once the people became convinced that Jesus was the Anointed One they had been waiting for, their next move was to make him king. Isn't it interesting that this wasn't actually the purpose that the Messiah was sent for? This was their long-awaited expectation—that the Messiah would come and that he would overthrow the governments of the earth. Yet this was not the desire of God. While the power structures we value are often enforcers, this is not how the kingdom of God works.

Think about your own desire for justice. What do you think has to change in order for systems to be made right? Often, God leads us on the humble path, the ordinary path, to experience true freedom. We cannot brandish weapons in the name of God and expect him to leave his place with the vulnerable. He will not be found protecting himself in halls of privilege. Jesus is with those who are suffering. Will we choose to meet him there?

*Jesus, I don't want to presume to put you in places you don't want to be. I honor you as you are, and that is often outside of my expectations, the systems I know, and the plans I make.*

# Keep Going

> After waiting until evening for Jesus to return, the disciples went down to the lake. But as darkness fell, he still hadn't returned, so the disciples got into a boat and headed across the lake to Capernaum.
>
> JOHN 6:16–17

Just as the disciples decided to keep going on their journey when Jesus didn't show up as expected, we can do the same. We are never far away from him. He will find us no matter where we go. If you have been waiting for permission to do what you have felt pulled to do, this is it. If you have been hesitating about taking the next steps because you need a sign from God, then do as the disciples did and just do the next thing.

God is gracious, and so are his ways. We don't have to figure everything out perfectly. In fact, there's no way that we can. Once we embrace this, there is incredible freedom for us to move through life, try and fail, and discover that Jesus meets us still.

*Gracious Jesus, thank you for the permission to keep going when I can't sense you. I don't have to sit in one spot waiting for your return. You will meet me on my way. Thank you.*

# Waves of Doubt

> By now a strong wind began to blow and was stirring up the waters. The disciples had rowed about halfway across the lake when all of a sudden they caught sight of Jesus walking on top of the waves, coming toward them. The disciples panicked.
>
> JOHN 6:18–19

Can you imagine what the disciples must have felt in this moment? They had waited for Jesus to return to the shore, but when it started getting dark, they made the decision to cross the lake. Perhaps when the wind began to blow and stir up the waters, their doubts also began to stir. Should they really have left without him?

Doubt can lead to fear, which can quickly lead us into panic. Once we're in that place, our normal, rational thinking gives way to worst-case scenarios and a survival mindset. When the disciples spotted Jesus walking on top of the waves, they did not recognize him. Fear kept them from seeing that the One they had been waiting for had met them in the middle of the lake. When doubt and fear start raging within you, take a deep breath, focus on where your feet meet the floor, and ask for Jesus to reveal where he is in the moment.

*Jesus, when doubt crowds my mind and clouds my ability to see you clearly, announce yourself. I welcome you.*

# Don't Be Afraid

Jesus called out to them, "Don't be afraid.
You know who I am."

JOHN 6:20

J esus is a safe place. His disciples were huddled in fear in the middle of their boat in the midst of a storm. When Jesus walked on top of the waves to meet them, their fear grew. That is, until Jesus spoke. His words, "Don't be afraid. You know who I am," must have brought relief.

Identify the fears and insecurities that are being stirred up in your life. As you do, take each one and speak Jesus' words over them. Don't leave out any. Perhaps this is a practice you can do throughout your day, any time you feel the fear or doubt clenching in your chest. Slow down, breathe deeply, and repeat Jesus' words. It doesn't matter how often it happens; practice meeting your fear with Jesus' truth. He meets you in the middle of your storm even as he met the disciples in theirs.

*Prince of Peace, thank you for your persistent presence. Bring calm and courage to my heart, especially as I speak your words over my circumstances.*

# Present Relief

They were relieved to take him in, and the moment Jesus stepped into the boat, they were instantly transported to the other side!

JOHN 6:21

Jesus' presence brought tremendous relief to the disciples' hearts. Have you ever felt this way? Maybe a reliable friend or parent showed up right when you were getting desperate to figure out what to do. Perhaps you felt the peace of wisdom wash over you in a moment of indecision. You can feel the relief of someone's presence in myriad ways, and they are each a gift of peace.

Jesus did even more than bring peace to the disciples' worries and fears, but as soon as he entered the boat, they found themselves transported. There was no more work to do, no storm to wait out—nothing. Jesus' presence brought peace and solutions. It was miraculous. When we take Jesus into our hearts in the midst of our storm, he knows exactly what to do. He takes over and provides even more relief than simply his company. What a wonderful Savior!

*Jesus, your presence brings clarity and peace. Thank you for doing more than I expect whenever you come to my rescue.*

# Search for Him

When the people saw on the shoreline a number of small boats from Tiberias and realized Jesus and the disciples weren't there, they got into the boats and went to Capernaum to search for him. When they finally found him, they asked him, "Teacher, how did you get here?"

JOHN 6:24–25

After Jesus and his disciples were already gone from the other side of the lake, the people noticed. They went to Capernaum to search for him. Remember, these were the same people who wanted to make Jesus their king. We know that many of these people did not follow Jesus very much longer, and perhaps this is why Jesus seems to be losing patience with them.

He knew their hearts beyond their questions. He knew that they loved his miracles but that they didn't really want to embrace his ways. It is never a bad thing to pursue Christ. We should let our desire lead us to him. Once we meet him, are we ready for his answers to our questions? We must allow our hearts to remain open to his teachings even when we don't understand at first. He feeds the hungry, gives wisdom to the humble, and faithfully leads his followers.

*Jesus, open my understanding to receive your teachings. I want to know you as you are, not how I think you are.*

# He Knows Our Hearts

Jesus replied, "Let me make this very clear, you came looking for me because I fed you by a miracle, not because you believe in me."

JOHN 6:26

Depending on our motivations, knowing that Jesus sees through to our hearts may either bring relief or worry. In the end, we can hide nothing from God. This is actually wonderful news. This means he cannot be fooled by anyone. He sees through to the heart of a person, and that is why it is his job alone to be the judge.

It is good to question our own motives from time to time. Why we feel drawn to respond in certain ways may reveal insecurities, desires, or unmet needs. Jesus has so much compassion for us; we also must learn to be compassionate with ourselves. Even if we first came to follow Christ because of signs and wonders, or anything other than belief in him as Son of God, we have the opportunity to realign in his mercy. He knows our hearts, so why not give all that we are to know his heart? What we find is worth more than the wealth of this world could afford.

*Son of God, I believe that you are good, you are powerful, and you are alive. I believe that you are worthy of my submission and my trust. You have it.*

# *What Matters Most*

> "Why would you strive for food that is perishable and not be passionate to seek the food of eternal life, which never spoils? I, the Son of Man, am ready to give you what matters most, for God the Father has destined me for this purpose."
>
> JOHN 6:27

We can spend our days striving for things that quickly lose their satisfaction, or we can choose to go after that which matters most. Christ offers us the latter. How many of us have felt fulfilled in our jobs, relationships, and so on, only to wake up one day feeling like we would change it all? Our lives have natural ebbs and flows. We will not always be happy. Things will not always be easy, and we have to learn how to persevere.

Jesus is not offering us an escape route from the dissatisfaction we feel with life. He is offering us himself. We will still go through trials, have health issues, and have tension in our relationships. In the midst of all of it, we have his powerful presence and his promise. We have his persistent peace, overwhelming joy, and constant love. Even more, we know that those who believe in him "will never perish but experience everlasting life" (John 3:16). What a hope!

*Jesus, revive the passion in my heart to know you more.*

## Starting Point

They replied, "So what should we do if we want to do God's work?" Jesus answered, "The work you can do for God starts with believing in the One he has sent."

JOHN 6:28–29

Jesus gave a very clear starting point for doing the work of God: "Believing in the One he has sent." If we truly believe that Jesus is the Christ, the Savior, and the Son of God, then we will follow his teachings, adopt his ways, and believe his promises. No one has more authority under God than Jesus!

If we want to do God's work, whether in our own lives, our communities, or the larger world, then the place to begin is always believing in Christ. We must develop devotion in our lives as we grow closer to him. We need to make sure that we don't just say we believe in him but that we also practice what he clearly preached. His words bring life and understanding to the seeking heart. He always knows what we need right when we need it, and we should not hesitate to bring our questions to him. It's all about developing a living relationship with Christ through his Spirit that dwells with us.

*Jesus, I believe that you are the Son of God and that your life, teachings, and resurrection all point to the wisdom and love of God the Father. Thank you.*

# Bread of Life

Jesus said to them, "I am the Bread of Life.
Come every day to me and you will never be hungry.
Believe in me and you will never be thirsty."

JOHN 6:35

Jesus described himself to the woman at the well as "Living Water." Now, sometime later, he describes himself to the people who came after him as "the Bread of Life." In Christ, we have all the nourishment our souls need. He offers more than practical needs (though he is good at providing those for us). He offers us the food and water of his presence.

As we come to him every day, our souls and spirits are filled. He gives us the daily supply to satisfy our hunger. We cannot hoard this food. We come to him, and he offers us a fresh portion each time. We will never thirst or hunger for deeper meaning or purpose when we remain filled up on Jesus, our Living Water and Bread of Life. We must not neglect coming to him every day, for he is our perfect portion for every circumstance and in every moment.

*Lord, you are the one I come to for soul nourishment and satisfaction. I believe that you have all I need, so please fill me up, Lord.*

## *Embraced by God*

"Everyone my Father has given to me, they will come. And all who come to me, I will embrace and will never turn them away."

JOHN 6:37

Do you know how deeply God loves you? He knows you best, better than your closest friends, family members, and even better than you know yourself. You were created for intimate relationship with God. Come to God, and you will find yourself embraced by the King of kings.

Jesus never turns away those who come to him, and the only thing keeping you from him may be yourself. Does shame pull you to remain at a distance? Beloved, he already knows you through and through. You cannot shock him. He is not waiting with a lecture but with open arms. Think of the parable of the prodigal son. God celebrates your coming (no matter how little or often) with a hearty embrace and pure love and forgiveness. Don't hesitate a moment longer!

*Jesus, I will not stay at a distance today. I come to you even if it is a slow crawl to get there. I bring all that I am. Receive me, Lord, and wrap me in your loving embrace.*

# The Father's Longing

"The longing of my Father is that everyone who embraces the
Son and believes in him will experience eternal life and I will raise
them up in the last day!"

JOHN 6:40

Your understanding of the Father informs your ideas of
God's nature. When you picture the Father, what kind
of disposition do you think he has? Perhaps you think he is
aloof, vengeful, or unpredictable. Maybe you already see him
the way Jesus presented him: as the loving Father. Jesus' idea
of the Father was based in utter truth. He didn't exaggerate
or diminish a thing. Jesus knows the Father best, and we can
trust that what he says is true.

God longs to usher you into his kingdom where you will
dwell with him forever. The love of Jesus is not distinct to
him; the love of Jesus is a reflection of the love of the Father.
He wants all people to experience the freedom and power
of his mercy in their lives. You don't have to wonder what
the Father feels toward you. He loves you. Not "he loves you
except for." Not "he loves you in spite of." He loves you. Be
drawn to his love and let him revive your hope today.

*Father, open my understanding to see you as you truly are:
merciful, kind, and better than I can imagine.*

## *Drawn to Jesus*

"The only way people come to me is by the Father who sent me—
he pulls on their hearts to embrace me. And those who are drawn
to me, I will certainly raise them up in the last day."

JOHN 6:44

When you feel something pulling on your heart today, turn toward it. When compassion draws you, don't dismiss it. Jesus Christ is still working in your life, and he has not abandoned you. However small the turning, every movement matters.

In the presence of Christ, you can let down all of your defenses. You have no need to protect yourself against his kindness. He will not trick you, nor will he lead you down a path he is not already on. He goes with you wherever he leads. In Jesus, you will find your heart filled with comfort, hope, and peace. In him, you will be transformed to walk in his ways. His love is the purest source you will ever find. Let the King of kings pluck at the strings of your heart, and you will learn to dance to the song of the Lamb.

*Great God, thank you for drawing me to you. You started this work, and I trust you to continue it. I love you.*

# Taught by God

Jesus continued, "It has been written by the prophets, 'They will all be taught by God himself.' If you are really listening to the Father and learning directly from him, you will come to me. For I am the only One who has come from the Father's side, and I have seen the Father!"

JOHN 6:45–46

Isaiah 54:13 says, "All your children will be taught by Yahweh, and great will be their peace." No better teacher exists than God himself, and he promised to instruct us. Jesus is the incarnation of God, teaching us the ways of God's kingdom. God himself came to earth to show us what he is like.

The invitation to be taught by God still remains today. Through Jesus' words, life, and ministry, we can see what is most important to God. The fellowship of the Holy Spirit imparts revelations of God's character to our hearts, making the knowledge of God go deeper than our cognitive understanding. His ways are peaceful, not volatile. His nature is constant even while the world changes around us. We have so much to learn from him beyond what we have yet grasped, and he teaches us himself when we humble ourselves as students and disciples before him.

*Jesus, teach me your ways. Show me the wonders of God's kingdom. I am open.*

## *United Heart*

"I speak to you living truth: Unite your heart to me and believe—
and you will experience eternal life!"

JOHN 6:47

When we unite our hearts with another's, we join in purpose as well as in intimate connection. It is a beautiful thing to unite our hearts to Jesus' heart. It is no small thing, though. Jesus is trustworthy. He will not fail us. We can put our total hope in him, joining our hearts with his wonderful love. There is nothing better in this world!

Abundant life is found in fellowship with Christ. He offers us the fullness of his kingdom and its resources. When we are tired, we find rest. When we are weak, we lean on his strength. When we run dry, he pours over us with the refreshing waters of his presence. Every experience we have of the Lord's goodness in our lives is but a tiny glimpse of the glory of his kingdom. We only see and taste in part now, but in eternity, there will be no more limits.

*Jesus, I unite my heart to you in faith, and I give you access to all of me. I believe that with you, my life becomes richer, my hope becomes greater, and my joy becomes deeper. Thank you.*

# Spirit Life

> "The Holy Spirit is the one who gives life, that which is of the natural realm is of no help. The words I speak to you are Spirit and life. But there are still some of you who won't believe."
>
> JOHN 6:63

The truth of faith is that we need the Holy Spirit in order to truly see, understand, and believe. The words of Jesus were full of the life of the Spirit, and that made them living and active. When the Spirit reveals the truth of God's Word to the hungry hearts of those who listen, transformation begins to take place.

It is the Holy Spirit's job, not ours, to draw people to Christ. He does the hidden work in people's hearts to draw them to Jesus. This means that we don't have to convince anyone. We can live the truth, sharing what is ours to share, and then leave the rest to the Holy Spirit. We do not have to feel as if we need to save anyone; that's not our job. Our job is to testify to Jesus' love and point others to him—not only with our words but also with our mercy, integrity, and peace.

*Holy Spirit, thank you for moving in the deep spaces of my heart, revealing the truth and power of Christ. I yield to you, and I allow you to do what only you can do in others.*

# Revelation of Eternal Life

Jesus said to his twelve, "And you—do you also want to leave?"
Peter spoke up and said, "But Lord, where would we go?
No one but you gives us the revelation of eternal life."

JOHN 6:67–68

Masses of followers had just abandoned Jesus. They could not embrace that he was the Son of God. In their offense, they turned their backs on him and refused any association with him (v. 66). Turning to his closest friends, the twelve disciples, Jesus asked them if they would do the same. Even in this question, we see the beautiful humanity of Christ as well as the invitation for his friends to choose for themselves what they would do.

Have you had a revelation of eternal life through Christ? Perhaps you have had a glimpse of his kindness, redeeming something in your life that you thought was forever lost. Maybe a miracle of his mercy has touched you. Even if all you have is the deep conviction of God's goodness, that is more than enough to keep going, is it not? Make your home in Christ, and he will be your anchor.

*Christ, even when I question the systems built around you, I don't have any desire to abandon you. You are my home.*

## Confession of Faith

"We're fully convinced that you are the Anointed One,
the Son of the Living God, and we believe in you!"

JOHN 6:69

The confession of our faith is a powerful thing. We don't have to declare it to everyone we cross paths with, but it is certainly important that we do it to the Lord. When we confess with our mouths that Jesus is Lord and believe in our hearts that God raised him from the dead, Romans 10:9 says we will experience salvation.

What we believe, we will confess. These two go hand in hand. If we live with integrity, being honest in our words and dealings, then it will be clear what our guiding values are. There is no need for hiding our conviction, and still it is such a personal thing. We cannot force anyone else to believe as we do, but we can certainly choose for ourselves and stand strong in Christ. Even when our beliefs change as our understanding deepens, Christ has no need to change. As we shed false ideas of what God is like and what our duty is, we take on the truth of his lordship over our lives.

*Jesus Christ, I believe that you are the Anointed One. I believe that you rose from the dead and are my Savior. I choose to follow you.*

## Differing Motivations

Jesus' brothers came to advise him, saying, "Why don't you leave the countryside villages and go to Judea where the crowds are, so that your followers can see your miracles?...How do you expect to be successful and famous if you do all these things in secret? Now is your time—go to Jerusalem, come out of hiding, and show the world who you are!"

JOHN 7:3–4

Jesus' brothers thought they knew what was best for him. They encouraged him to go to Judea so that he could gain more success and notability before greater groups of people. All the Jews would be gathered for the Feast of Tabernacles in Jerusalem. Wouldn't it make sense for Jesus to go?

While his brothers pushed Jesus to come out of hiding, he could see what they couldn't. Has anyone ever pushed you to do something before you were ready? Perhaps they had good intentions, but they dismissed your concerns. Timing is important, and we won't miss out on what is for us by rushing into something before we are ready. Only we can choose what we will do, and we can trust Jesus to guide us and to teach us to trust our intuition.

*Jesus, thank you for guiding me with your Spirit and for giving me intuition. Teach me how to tune in to that and tune others out when their advice is not right.*

# Not Yet

Jesus responded, "My time of being unveiled hasn't yet come, but any time is a suitable opportunity for you to gain man's approval. The world can't hate you, but it does me, for I am exposing their evil deeds."

JOHN 7:6–7

Jesus stood firm in his convictions and refused to be swayed by his brothers. He knew what he would encounter in Jerusalem while his brothers would not have to face the same thing. It is well and good for others to advise us, but if they won't experience what we likely will, then we should trust our own instincts more than others' arguments. Even when others have our best at heart, it does not mean we need to do as they think we should.

When you feel a *not yet* from the Lord, don't be afraid to wait patiently as he is calling you to do. Stand your ground. No one else has to understand it. Your family may not quite get why you would choose not to act, but just as Jesus waited on his Father's yes, it is good for you to wait on the Lord. Not every opportunity is a clear yes or no. Jesus knew that it wasn't his time, and you can learn to recognize the cues from your whole self—soul, spirit, and body.

*Jesus, thank you for the example you set. Teach me to know the timing of important matters.*

## Secret Journey

Jesus lingered in Galilee until his brothers had left for the feast in Jerusalem. Then later, Jesus took a back road and went into Jerusalem in secret.

JOHN 7:9–10

This verse is astonishing. Jesus had just finished telling his brothers that he would in no way go to Jerusalem with them to celebrate the feast. Yet here Jesus was a little while later, sneaking into Jerusalem on his own. Have you ever felt impatient and eager to gauge what was going on without you? Apparently, so did Jesus. He knew he couldn't come openly to Judea because he would be persecuted. Yet he still found a way to come on his own terms.

Some of us cannot return to familiar places because it feels too risky. Yet here in Jesus' example, we see another way. Is there a creative way possible that we can venture where we long to go even if we know that it isn't the right time to do it boldly? Perhaps you have never considered the possibility of entering a space in this way. Take time to pray and ask the Lord if this is something that you could do.

*Jesus, help me to know when I should wait and when I should follow a back road. I trust you, both in my public and secret journeys.*

# *Astonishing Wisdom*

> Not until the feast was half over did Jesus finally appear in the temple courts and begin to teach. The Jewish leaders were astonished by what he taught and said, "How did this man acquire such knowledge? He wasn't trained in our schools—who taught him?"
>
> JOHN 7:14–15

After lying low for a while, Jesus decided it was the right time to teach in the temple courts of Jerusalem. There he taught with such astonishing wisdom that the Jewish leaders and teachers felt perplexed about where he had obtained it. The wisdom of God is beyond our systems and logic, and yet it speaks to natural and supernatural order.

If you are looking for wisdom and insight today, look to Jesus. He holds the keys to wisdom, and he will unlock your understanding. Sit at his feet, read his Word, and spend time in prayer fellowshiping with his Spirit. Don't just talk to him, but also take time to listen for his reply. He longs to reveal his wisdom to you as you look to him.

*Jesus, as I come to you today, I ask you to open my heart to understand your words, your ways, and your nature in deeper ways. Show me something new about you that I don't yet realize.*

# The Highest Teacher

Jesus responded, "I don't teach my own ideas,
but the truth revealed to me by the One who sent me."

JOHN 7:16

Everything that Jesus did was what he saw the Father doing. Everything he taught was what the Father had revealed to him. He did nothing on his own. This is beautiful. He was so connected to his Father, and the Spirit so connected to them both, that they were in perfect unity in all that they did. This is still true.

When we don't know where to turn, we can turn to Christ. The truth he taught is the truth that still rings out from the Father. Malachi 3:6 says, "I the LORD do not change" (NCV). Our own understanding of God may, and most certainly will, change. We are constantly learning! "Jesus, the Anointed One," Hebrews 13:8 says, "is always the same—yesterday, today, and forever." God's character doesn't change, nor does his faithfulness. Let's stand, then, upon the firm foundation of his truth and trust him to guide us in our understanding.

*Jesus Christ, thank you for your wisdom that transcends my current understanding. You see what I cannot, and you lovingly guide me in your clarity. I follow you. All the way, Lord, I follow you.*

# *Passion for God's Will*

> "If you want to test my teachings and discover where I received them, first be passionate to do God's will, and then you will be able to discern if my teachings are from the heart of God or from my own opinions."
>
> JOHN 7:17

Have you ever found yourself in an argument in which your only goal was to make others hear your point? Once you stop listening and being open to hearing their perspective, your motive becomes to win or to shut them down. When the Pharisees wanted to test Jesus' teachings, it was with the same kind of motive. Most of them just wanted to prove Christ wrong. They weren't actually hungry to do the will of God.

Think through the interactions you have had with those around you. Now think through how you would like others to treat you in conversation. Do they match up? Today is a good day to make sure you have your motivations and priorities straight. In your conversations, instead of trying to shut others down with your opinions (even if you believe your perspective to be the right one), choose, instead, to take the way of Christ. Leave room for real conversation. Listen to others. Ask questions. And humbly provide your own perspective when asked.

*Jesus, help me seek your will and humbly listen to what others have to say.*

# *Pure Motives*

"Charlatans praise themselves and seek honor from men, but my Father sent me to speak truth on his behalf. And I have no false motive, because I seek only the glory of God."

JOHN 7:18

Jesus had no selfish ambition. Even more accurately, Jesus had only the will of God as his motive because he was one with his Father. He was his Dad's kid. Who of us has not seen the character traits of parents passed on to their children? Jesus' cares were the Father's cares and vice versa.

Jesus was about his Father's business, and his Father's business was motivated by pure love. When love is our motivation, we don't praise ourselves. When mercy is our inspiration, we don't need to seek the approval of others. Love compels us to reach out to others, all because we know how loved by God we all are. What glory God receives when we aim to please him rather than to catch the attention and praise of others.

*Lord, thank you for loving us with purity. Thank you, Jesus, that you did not, and still don't, have any desire to win others over with inauthenticity. I live for your glory, for it is better than living in the trap of trying to please others.*

# *Beyond the Superficial*

"Stop judging based on the superficial.
First you must embrace the standards of mercy and truth."

JOHN 7:24

The law of mercy overrides the laws of Moses. When Jesus healed the lame man on the Sabbath, he put the mercy-heart of God above the regulations of the Sabbath. When we look beyond the superficial, seeing situations and people through the lens of mercy, only then will we have true discernment.

In this world, it is common to judge others based on superficial criteria. From clothing to language to which traditions we keep—you name it, and we probably have a judgment about it. But this is not what Jesus taught or calls any of us to do. We must embrace the standards of mercy and truth that he set forth. We need to follow him on the pathway of his practical love, and then we will see even more clearly that Jesus is full of compassion. As James (Jacob) 2:13 puts it, "By showing mercy, you take dominion over judgment."

*Merciful One, I am so guilty of judging others, as well as myself, on superficial standards. I know that you are better than that. Teach me how to walk in your mercy and to look past the surface.*

# Lack of Understanding

"How could he be, since we know this man is from Galilee,
but no one will know where the true Messiah comes from,
he'll just appear out of nowhere."

JOHN 7:27

Because they knew where he grew up, some of the residents of Jerusalem could not wrap their heads around Jesus being the long-awaited Anointed One. They could not imagine the Messiah in flesh and blood being birthed by a woman and growing up in a normal household and in a normal way. Yet, beautifully, this is how the Messiah came to them—a humble man, the Son of God, and the anticipated Savior.

Have others ever underestimated you because of boxes people put you in? Even the Son of Man knows this feeling. Where you come from doesn't matter. The resources that were available—or, in some cases, unavailable—do not define your purpose. You were born with purpose. Don't let those who can't fathom your potential discourage you. Don't let your own humble beginnings define your future. Follow the Lord, and he will lead you into wholeness of heart and of purpose.

*Messiah, even though you came to Israel in an unexpected way, I, for one, am glad of it. You were from humble beginnings, and you persevered through hard times. I will follow you anywhere.*

## Faithful Father

Knowing all of this, Jesus one day preached boldly in the temple courts, "So, you think you know me and where I come from? But you don't know the One who sent me—the Father who is always faithful. I have not come simply on my own initiative."

JOHN 7:28

The mercy of God is undeniable in Jesus' life and ministry. He did what he saw the Father doing, and yet so many of the religious elite could not recognize the fingerprint of God on his life. What an indictment this was on their understanding. What a criticism it still is in many religious circles. Many today call on the name of Jesus and yet do horrible things in his name. They do not know the very one they claim to follow.

The Father is faithful, and so is Jesus. They will one day judge everything rightly and put justice into place on the earth. Until then, we are called to follow Christ's ways. We are to be merciful, to intervene on behalf of the vulnerable, and to care for others the way we should care for ourselves. We are not to scream judgments at anyone, for that does not reflect the goodness of God as displayed through Christ. He is full of patience, peace, and truth. He is kind and just. He is better than many of us give him credit for being.

*Faithful Father, thank you for the power of your love in this world and in my life. I submit to you.*

# From His Presence

"The Father has sent me here, and I know all about him,
for I have come from his presence."

JOHN 7:29

The people we know the best are those we spend the most time with. Jesus came from the presence of the Father. As the first chapter of John says, "In the beginning the Living Expression was already there…[he] was with God, yet fully God. They were together—face-to-face, in the very beginning" (vv. 1–2). Jesus Christ was more familiar with the Father than anyone else had ever been. He knew the Father because they were dwelling together in perfect unity.

If we want to know what God is truly like, we have to look no further than Jesus Christ. He is the Son of God, and he still reveals the heart of the Father to those who look to him. The Spirit of God brings the presence of God. We are never without it. We can get to know this God for ourselves through fellowship with Christ. What better way is there to know God than to spend time with him in his presence?

*Lord Jesus, I believe that you are with the Father now and that you are also with me through your Spirit. Thank you for the power of your presence. I want to know you more.*

## *Limited Time*

Jesus said, "My days to be with you are numbered.
Then I will return to the One who sent me.
And you will search for me and not be able to find me."

JOHN 7:33–34

Just as Jesus' days were limited on the earth, so are ours. When we have a sense of this, we can more purposefully live out our days. Youth makes us think we are invincible, but when we truly face our own mortality—whether through the loss of a loved one, an illness, war, or a global crisis—suddenly the trivial things don't seem to matter as much. All of a sudden, we become more focused. We don't have to go looking for these opportunities. They will come to each of us.

When we live with a deep purpose, even if it is as simple as loving the ones around us well, we can focus in without letting the distractions of life rob us of our time. We have to make the choices to do what is important. We must be the ones who make changes, in our mindsets and lifestyles, to live with more intention. Today, let's consider what truly matters to us and make more time for those things, cutting away the excess if need be.

*Jesus, help me to really seize what is important and to let go of the things that don't matter. I want to live with intentionality, not as if life is just happening to me.*

# Rivers of Living Water

On the most important day of the feast, the last day, Jesus stood and shouted out to the crowds—"All you thirsty ones, come to me! Come to me and drink! Believe in me so that rivers of living water will burst out from within you, flowing from your innermost being, just like the Scripture says!"

JOHN 7:37–38

When we drink from the presence of Jesus, a sip becomes a river. What powerful imagery this is! It is indicative of the Holy Spirit. Jesus was preparing the peoples' hearts to receive the outpouring of the Spirit, which would come later. But that later has already come for us. We don't need to wait to receive the Spirit, for as we come to Christ, he freely pours out his Spirit on all who believe in him.

Rivers of living water flow in the presence of God today. These refreshing waters will rejuvenate your heart, body, and mind. They will burst from within you like a river gushing from the side of a mountain. The purest Source endlessly fills you with the purity of his presence, and it can't help but overflow. Fill up in his presence, and you will have more than enough to flow into every area of your life. It doesn't cost a thing to drink up (see Isaiah 55:1).

*Jesus, I do believe in you. Let rivers of your living waters flood me from within.*

# *Impressed by Jesus*

They answered, "You don't understand—he speaks amazing
things like no one else has ever spoken!"

JOHN 7:46

The religious leaders had divided opinions about who
Jesus was. While many wanted him silenced, still others
could not shake the influence of his powerful teachings. The
temple guards, returning to the leading priests empty-handed,
were reprimanded for not bringing Jesus back with them.
These guards were impressed by him, yet many of the Pharisees
believed the reason why the temple guards were attracted to
Jesus' teachings was their ignorance of the law.

When offense lines our hearts, we will make excuses
for why we are right and others are wrong. This is clearly
the effect of pride. And yet how exhausting it is to feel so
enraged all the time! We should lean in with curiosity to
the areas where blinding anger leads us and the areas where
we are open to reconsideration. Love leads with gentleness,
kindness, and a willingness to listen. Fear tries to keep us
insulated and self-protective.

*Jesus, I lay down before you today the areas of offense in
my own heart. Help me to walk in the path of your love, the
humble way of your example. I choose you over my own
reactive pride. Your love liberates, while fear shuts us in.*

# Blinded to Their History

They argued, "Oh, so now you're an advocate for this Galilean!
Search the Scriptures, Nicodemus, and you'll see that there's no
mention of a prophet coming out of Galilee!"

JOHN 7:52

None of us knows the full picture, not even of our own history. We all have blind spots, and this is so very important to recognize. If we are willing to admit that we only know and see in small parts, then we can remain open to learning as we grow. Life is a never-ending opportunity to mature. This means that we will often get it wrong. We must learn to keep a humble heart that does better when we know better.

The Pharisees were convinced that they knew the Scriptures, as well as their history, better than Jesus. We know that they were wrong. This is easy to see through the lens of hindsight, where our own biases and beliefs are not challenged. It is much harder to recognize where our own theologies have been limiting the expansive truth of God. May we remain softhearted, open, and willing to do the work of restoration, reconciliation, and humility when presented with the opportunity.

*Jesus, I humble myself before you. I am willing to admit that there is so much I don't know. I don't want to be stubborn to your correction. Open my eyes today.*

# Caught in the Act

> Then in the middle of his teaching, the religious scholars and the
> Pharisees broke through the crowd and brought a woman who
> had been caught in the act of committing adultery and made her
> stand in the middle of everyone.
>
> JOHN 8:3

The Pharisees dragged the accused woman before Jesus, bringing her all alone in her humiliation even though there was obviously someone else to share in her shame. Interesting that the Pharisees would let her lover go and still demand punishment for her. Have you ever been singled out for something that you did not do alone? How did it make you feel?

We do not need help in feeling shame. Not only was this woman fully humiliated, being dragged into the temple courts among a crowd, but her life was also at stake. Moses' law, the Pharisees pointed out, commanded them to stone such a person. They were quick to make a black-and-white statement about God's will and ways. Thankfully, Jesus did not condone such behavior. Even when we are filled with shame, God does not condemn us. He meets us with mercy.

*Merciful One, I don't want to get so caught up in the rules of what is right and wrong that I miss my brother or sister's humanity. Melt my heart in your mercy.*

# Quiet Answers of Truth

"Doesn't Moses' law command us to stone to death a woman like this? Tell us, what do you say we should do with her?" They were only testing Jesus because they hoped to trap him with his own words and accuse him of breaking the laws of Moses. But Jesus didn't answer them. Instead he simply bent down and wrote in the dust with his finger.

JOHN 8:5–6

We cannot trap God, not even by using his own Word. The religious leaders of Jesus' day tried and failed many times. They thought they knew better than Jesus, and their hard hearts only wanted to prove him wrong.

Jesus did not meet their indignation with his own. Instead, he bent down and wrote his reply in the dust. We do not know for certain what it is he wrote, but we do know that it disarmed the angry mob. Jesus knew each of those men. He could see their hearts, and he knew their motivations. He could tell they only wanted to trap him. It was wisdom that led him to quietly respond. Have you ever diffused an argument with a quiet but firm response? Try to follow Jesus' lead today and do just that when others come at you with demands for something you are not willing to give.

*Lord, help me to stand in truth and grace, undeterred by the indignation of others.*

## No One Is Perfect

Angry, they kept insisting that he answer their question, so Jesus stood up and looked at them and said, "Let's have the man who has never had a sinful desire throw the first stone at her."

JOHN 8:7

We live in a world filled with criticism and judgments. Perfectionism tells us that if only we try harder, we can have it all. Perfectionism is not the way of Christ or his kingdom. We criticize others all the while overlooking our own flaws and faults. None of us is without sin. We all fall short of the glory of God. It is important to recognize our humanity so that we don't overvalue ourselves and undervalue others.

Christ did not say "the man who appears to have no sin" could throw a stone at the woman. The Greek word used for *sin* in this context can best be translated as "a sinful desire." Who has never had a sinful desire? Even if we don't act on it, we all have moments of temptation. Why would we condemn someone else for losing the same fight? Instead of judging others to destruction, we should encourage them in the liberty of Christ.

*Savior, thank you for being strong in mercy and quick in forgiveness. Help me to be just like you even when it is not the popular opinion.*

# *Holy Conviction*

Upon hearing that, her accusers slowly left the crowd
one at a time, beginning with the oldest to the youngest,
with a convicted conscience.

JOHN 8:9

Conviction is not the same as shame. Conviction shows us the truth of our hearts while shame distorts our worth. Conviction does not condemn our identity; it reveals our flaws. Shame is a heavy-handed abuser that tries to convince us that our mistakes make us unlovable.

The accusers left one by one, dropping their stones as they did. No one could accuse the woman after being confronted by Jesus' words, both spoken and written. Jesus knows how to pierce our hearts when we need a reality check. He does not shy away from speaking the truth, and he also does not submit to the pressure of the priests who thought they knew better. Just as he stood his ground in truth and mercy, so can we.

*Jesus, I don't know what you wrote in the dirt, but I do know that you revealed truth that convicted these men's hearts. May I be free from shame but full of conviction when you speak words of correction to me.*

## Pardoned by Love

> Until finally, Jesus was left alone with the woman still standing there in front of him. So he stood back up and said to her, "Dear woman, where are your accusers? Is there no one here to condemn you?" Looking around, she replied, "I see no one, Lord." Jesus said, "Then I certainly don't condemn you either. Go, and from now on, be free from a life of sin."
>
> JOHN 8:10–11

The woman had a powerful encounter with the love of Christ. Not only would he not condemn her, but he would not allow anyone else to either. In the Aramaic, there is a powerful testimony from this woman. She seemed to have had the revelation of who Jesus truly was, for she addressed him with the divine name MarYah, which means Lord YAHWEH.

When we are met with such mercy as this woman was, it is an extremely humbling yet liberating experience. Isn't it wonderful to know that Jesus won't condemn you to suffer under humiliation and abuse? He liberated her, *then* told her to be free from living a life of sin. Notice that this was after she had already been pardoned. May we take hold of the freedom that is ours and live for his glory.

*Messiah, thank you for your generous mercy. Help me to live it out in the way I treat others.*

# Life-Giving Light

Jesus said, "I am light to the world, and those who embrace me will experience life-giving light, and they will never walk in darkness."

JOHN 8:12

When we walk in the light of Christ, we will not be overcome by the darkness. He radiates light, and every shadow flees. What was once hidden by darkness is lit up by his presence. This is not something to be afraid of. It brings safety and security. It brings freedom and joy. It brings life.

In Psalm 56:13, King David talked about the life-giving light that Jesus described: "For you have saved my soul from death and my feet from stumbling so that I can walk before the Lord bathed in his life-giving light." Jesus is the Savior of our souls, and he clears the path so that we can walk in his gloriously satisfying presence. Why would we do anything but embrace him?

*Glorious One, thank you for leading me to the Father. Thank you for removing every barrier that stood between us. Thank you for defeating the power of sin and death. Thank you for saving me.*

# Knowing Who You Are

Jesus responded, "Just because I am the one making these claims doesn't mean they're invalid. For I absolutely know who I am, where I've come from, and where I'm going. But you Pharisees have no idea about what I'm saying."

JOHN 8:14

What would it change in your life if you never questioned your worth? Jesus knew where he came from, he knew who he was, and he knew where he was going. He wants the same for each of us. Every person is created in the image of the Creator. He wants what is best for you. He wants you to know who you are and where you've come from, and he wants you to have full confidence in his faithfulness.

Today is the day to throw off the judgments of others. Don't let someone who doesn't know you tear your identity apart. It can feel like a constant battle to dodge the accusations, misunderstandings, and judgments of others. When your identity is rooted in the peace, love, and purpose of God, you can keep coming back to that place of truth. Feel the weight of expectation fall off as you remember who you are and who God says you are.

*Creator, remind me who I am in you and who you are in me. Your opinion is more important than anyone else's.*

## So Much Better

"For you've set yourselves up as judges of others based on outward appearances, but I certainly never judge others in that way."

JOHN 8:15

Isn't it refreshing to know that Jesus does not judge us based on what we look like? He cares more about the posture of our hearts than he does about the way we present ourselves to the world. He loves us as much on the days when we can't even crawl out of bed as he does on our most productive days. God is so much better, so much more compassionate, so much kinder than we are with ourselves.

It is a beautiful practice to become more like Christ in our interactions with each other. When we might be quick to judge others based on what they look like, we can be intentional about seeing past that initial impression. Instead of just going with the first thought we have, let's do as Paul did and "capture…every thought and insist that it bow in obedience to the Anointed One" (2 Corinthians 10:5). As our thoughts bow to Christ, we can redirect our inner world to curiosity, compassion, and the leading of the Holy Spirit.

*Anointed One, you are so much better than anyone I've ever known. Renew my thoughts in your mercy and share your heart with me.*

# Testifying the Truth

> "Isn't it written in the law of Moses that the testimony of two men is trustworthy? Then what I say about who I am is true, for I am not alone in my testimony—my Father is the other witness, and we testify together of the truth."
>
> JOHN 8:17–18

The religious leaders did not understand what Jesus was saying about the Father witnessing and confirming his testimony. He did not say this and prove himself in the moment. He was speaking truth, but the hard-hearted would not believe him. It was only later, after he was crucified, resurrected, and returned to the Father, that the testimony was truly revealed. Even then, many refused to believe.

When we testify the truth, others may not quickly see the evidence. This does not mean that we should back down. We see this in the world. Many are quick to jump to judgment without due process. The truth will stand no matter how vehemently others deny it. The truth will come out; it always does. In the meantime, we must trust God the way Jesus trusted the Father, for he will not fail us.

*Holy One, thank you for knowing the truth about every circumstance even when others fail to see it. I trust you.*

## *From Above*

Jesus spoke up and said, "You are all from the earth; I am from above. I am not from this world like you are. That's why I've told you that you will all die in your sins if you fail to believe that I AM who I AM."

JOHN 8:23–24

If we truly want to walk in the wisdom, truth, and goodness of God, then we have no further to look than Jesus. His life, his teachings, his example, are reflective of who God is, for Jesus Christ was, is, and always will be God. No secret systems, no exclusive clubs, and no amount of money can guide us into deeper truth than what Jesus freely gives us. What a beautiful and liberating gift this is!

In John 14:6 Jesus said, "To know me is to know my Father too." It could not be clearer. We don't have to jump through any hoops, go on a pilgrimage to a far-off place, or shape-shift to others' expectations. We come freely to Christ, the One who is from above, and he receives us as we are. We offer ourselves as gifts to the One who knows us from the beginning of time. Anything we could ever give, he outdoes in loyal and extravagant offerings of his mercy toward us. How could we but worship this wonderful King?

*Jesus Christ, I give up my search for kingdom treasures outside of you. Thank you for fellowship that leads me into my liberation and deeper into your heart and perspective.*

## *Never Faltering*

They asked him plainly, "Who are you?"
"I am the One I've always claimed to be." Jesus replied.

JOHN 8:25

Jesus was clear about who he was from the beginning. He never changed his tune. The Jewish leaders could not comprehend what he was saying because they refused to believe that he could be the Anointed One. Many of them resisted his truth because it did not fit the narrative that they were expecting. They could not adjust their pride in order to truly receive what he was saying.

Perhaps you can relate to Jesus in this passage, especially when people misunderstand you or confront you with something that clearly is not true. People's expectations of us cannot be our foundation. We will disappoint and frustrate some, and that is no reason to change who we are. Perhaps you can relate to the Pharisees who wanted proof after proof, only to find fault in whatever was presented. The next time you ask something, choose to open your heart and mind and accept the answer for what it is.

*Lord, thank you for being my place of safety. My identity is rooted in who you say I am, and that is good. I trust you. Lead me in curiosity and in kindness and help me to be true to who I am and who you are.*

## Embrace the Truth

Jesus said to those Jews who believed in him, "When you continue to embrace all that I teach, you prove that you are my true followers. For if you embrace the truth, it will release true freedom into your lives."

JOHN 8:31–32

When we embrace the truth of Christ, it leads us into personal freedom. We are released from the mistakes of our past, the bondage of our sins, and the captivity of religion. We are free from the perfectionism and endless demands of human tradition. As we embrace the truth, we integrate it into our daily lives. There is no other way. Christ is our liberation. He is the reality of our freedom, and this is wonderful news!

No matter where this finds you today, consider it your invitation to embrace the truth of Christ—the reality of who he is—in your life. If you have been waiting for a less busy season to pursue his mercy, know that his love is not demanding. Come to him, receive what he has to offer, and drink deeply in his presence. He offers you more freedom today.

*Anointed One, I believe that you are the Truth, the reality of God in human form. I choose to come to you; release more freedom as I do.*

# Jesus, Our Emancipator

"I speak eternal truth," Jesus said. "When you sin you are not free. You've become a slave in bondage to your sin."

JOHN 8:34

Sin is a slave master, whereas Jesus unlocks our chains, frees us from its heavy burdens, and leads us into fields of opportunity. We have been invited to enjoy a life of freedom in Christ. Galatians 5:1 puts it this way: "At last we have freedom, for Christ has set us free! We must…firmly refuse to go back into the bondage of our past."

As humans, we are constantly looking for ways to feel in control of a world and in a life that is full of uncertainty. Yet if we hold too tightly, we will find ourselves tied to cycles and systems that oppress us. We must live in the freedom that Christ has offered us and refuse to go back to the bondage of sin. He has set us completely and wonderfully free, so let's embrace that liberty today and live for his glory.

*Rescuer, it is almost too much to grasp that you offer me full freedom from guilt, shame, and sin. Lift the weight that I have been carrying as I step back into the light of your gaze. I long for your refreshing love to revive me once again.*

# Unquestionably Free

"If the Son sets you free from sin,
then become a true son and be unquestionably free!"

JOHN 8:36

Embraced by love, we come alive. The Son of God, Jesus Christ, wraps us up in the mercy of God as we come to him. He frees us from the debt of sin, addiction, and fear. In the court of sin, he took our place and took the weight of our sentence. Why would we ever go back to a life of captivity when he offers us the liberty of his love?

How can you move from a place of being somewhat free in the mercy of Christ to being "unquestionably" free? The favor of God is not fame, fortune, or power. It is the kindness of God toward us. The most powerful gift he has given us is freedom from the obligation we had to sin. We are forever free in his love, and we get to choose how we will live that out. Choose, then, to be a true child of God and to live in the delight of his favor toward you.

*Savior, I am overwhelmed by the power of your kindness. You took the weight of my sin, my shame, and my rebellion, and you offered me freedom. What a beautiful gift this is! I want to live in this liberation in every area of my life.*

# Keep an Open Heart

Jesus said, "Then if God were really your father, you would love me, for I've come from his presence. I didn't come here on my own, but God sent me to you. Why don't you understand what I say? You don't understand because your hearts are closed to my message!"

JOHN 8:42–43

We reveal our values as we live out the fruit of them. The religious elite thought that they knew God, but what they really knew was the law of Moses. It is entirely possible to know Scripture well and still completely miss God moving in and around us. We cannot become so proud as to think we know all that there is to know about God and thereby close our hearts to learning and growing in understanding.

How can you practice keeping an open heart to God not only in your personal life but also in your community, in your interactions with others, and in your workplace? Wisdom's fruit can be identified with Spirit's discernment. We know what the fruit of the Spirit looks like, and if we look for it, we may just be surprised where we find it.

*Christ, thank you for the power of your love that is so far-reaching that it can't be contained. Open my heart and understanding to see where you are working around me today. I am willing.*

## *Prince of Truth*

> "I am the true Prince who speaks nothing but the truth, yet you refuse to believe and you want nothing to do with me."
>
> JOHN 8:45

The truth can be divisive. When we think we already know everything, we are closed off to learning. The Pharisees thought they knew God, yet they wanted nothing to do with Jesus. We see the error in their ways now, but would we have embraced Christ or rejected him if we lived in their time?

Some will refuse to recognize the truth, and we cannot change that. Others will embrace it. We can only affect our own reaction to the truth and engage others with an invitation to hear it. We cannot control what anyone else will do with it or dictate how they will react. Let's stop getting distracted by what others do or will do with the truth and instead take ownership over our own responses to it. That is all that we can do. It is the Holy Spirit who works in our hearts to draw us, so all we need to do is to be obedient to the Word of Christ over us.

*Jesus, thank you not only for telling the truth but for also being the Truth. I believe that you know better than I do, and you know better than even the most respected leaders I know.*

# *Fruit of Faith*

"If you really knew God, you would listen, receive, and respond with faith to his words. But since you don't listen and respond to what he says, it proves you don't belong to him and you have no room for him in your hearts."

JOHN 8:47

The response of trusting and believing in God is to listen to him, receive what he offers, and respond with faith to his words. If we claim to know him yet we ignore him, we fool ourselves. In order to make room for the Lord in our hearts, we must choose to humble ourselves before him. We must then do what he tells us to do.

The fruit of faith does not mean that life suddenly becomes easy. There will be hardships we will face, and we cannot avoid grief, suffering, or pain. Knowing God means knowing that he is with us through it all. It means inviting in his perspective when we cannot see. It means trusting that what he promises, he will deliver. It requires openness, adaptability, and resolute trust. It is not a chore but an honor, for he is so very faithful to us in love.

*Jesus, I won't just talk the talk, but I will walk it out. As I do, may the fruit of faith burst from my life. I trust you.*

# Curses Can't Stop Him

Jesus replied, "It is not a demon that would cause me to honor my Father. I live my life for his honor, even though you insult me for it."

JOHN 8:49

Insults and curses cannot deter the truth. If someone throws slurs at you, it does not actually change your identity, though it may sting. Can you imagine what Jesus must have felt when those who should have known him best ridiculed him? Even so, he is full of mercy to anyone who comes to him with a humble and seeking heart.

We all know that the best way to win someone's favor is to be kind. Deriding others does nothing but reveal the flaws in our own character. We all have bad days and moments of sheer pessimism. This was not the issue with the religious leaders confronting Christ, however. They were dedicated in their pursuit to bring him down. Even in the face of such insults, Jesus did not back down. Though it may hurt when others mock us, we do not live for their approval.

*Jesus, I want to live my life for your honor and for the opinion of the Father. Help me to stay rooted in you, unshakable in the face of insults.*

## *Joyous Revelations*

"Not only that, Abraham, your ancestor, was overjoyed when he received the revelation of my coming to earth. Yes, he foresaw me coming and was filled with delight!"

JOHN 8:56

The reality of a dream coming true may not feel as romantic as the buildup to it because we can't imagine things perfectly. Hope fills our expectations, but they do not account for the subtle differences, struggles, and humanity we cannot escape. It is good to be filled with delight at what is to come, but it is also important to recognize that it may look different from how we assume it will.

Many of the Jewish leaders of Jesus' time missed the Messiah right in front of them because they could not believe that he would come in such a way—a man from Nazareth. God humbling himself in human form, challenging their traditions, and choosing to extend mercy instead of judgment did not fit with their expectations. What joyful things do we look forward to? We must consider how we can loosen our expectations about the details.

*Lord, your ways are so thorough and purposeful. I trust that when you reveal what is to come, your details are better than any I can expect. I let go of the need to control any of it.*

# The I AM

Jesus said to them, "I give you this eternal truth:
I have existed long before Abraham was born, for I AM!"

JOHN 8:58

Even the most respected forefathers of the Jewish faith did not predate Christ. Even though many of the Jewish leaders doubted Jesus' identity, he did not shy away from saying who he was. The Jewish leaders were so offended at Jesus' statement that they picked up rocks to stone him.

It is important to know the state of our hearts. Will we be offended by the God of the Ages when he comes to us in unexpected form? Do we presume to know all that God will do in this world, how he shows up, and how he can move? We must remain humble and openhearted. The Spirit of God dwells in our midst, and he will give us discernment. Even more, we know the character of God. Pride leads to offense, and it keeps us from embracing God as he reveals himself. Today is the perfect opportunity to humble ourselves before the I AM. He can move in any way he wants, in any form, and through whomever he chooses. The fruit of his nature will always be the same.

*Lord, I recognize how little I truly know about you and your kingdom. As I draw near to you in truth and love, reveal yourself to me more and more.*

# Refrain from Judging

His disciples asked him, "Teacher, whose sin caused this guy's blindness, his own, or the sin of his parents?" Jesus answered, "Neither. It happened to him so that you could watch him experience God's miracle."

JOHN 9:2–3

Isn't it interesting that the disciples assumed a man's blindness was the direct result of sin in his life or in the life of his parents? Hopefully we don't walk around with these same judgments. Jesus clearly revealed that the man's blindness was not his fault. It was not sin that led to his disability. We must refrain from casting similar judgments on people who don't fit our idea of wholeness.

Jesus, full of gracious love, took this opportunity to reveal the heart of the Father through a miraculous intervention with this man. Jesus did not have biases against people who were different from him. We find how often he reached out to those with whom "respectable" Jewish men would not have interacted. Consider the negative mindsets from which you find it hard to break free. Now think about Jesus' example of what the Father is like. How does the Father's mercy shatter the biased ideas you hold?

*King of Kings, the way you always lead with love and kindness to the vulnerable astounds me. May I be just like you, Lord. Expand my understanding of who you are as I follow your example.*

# *Piercing Light*

"As long as I am with you my life is the light
that pierces the world's darkness."

JOHN 9:5

Jesus is the piercing light that brings clarity to the world's darkness. His life reveals the heart of the Father. His ministry shows how passionately God meets those who pursue him. There is so much goodness, freedom, and joy in the kingdom of Christ. There is more that we await in the abundance of his kingdom than we have experienced yet.

If you have felt clouded by the world's opinions, systems, and priorities, take some time in the presence of God today. He is the light that pierces the darkness. As you look to him, his light burns through the fog of your mind and reveals what is true. Fear recedes. Anxiety calms. His light brings peace. Find yourself at home in the peace of his presence and wait on his perspective to inform your own. He is good, and he will show up for you.

*Light of the World, brighten the darkness around me and reveal what has been hidden by the clouds of confusion. As I wait on you, rise like the dawn on my heart, mind, body, and soul.*

## Creative Healing

Jesus spat on the ground and made some clay with his saliva. Then he anointed the blind man's eyes with the clay. And he said to the blind man, "Now go and wash the clay from your eyes in the ritual pool of Siloam." So he went and washed his face and as he came back, he could see for the first time in his life!

JOHN 9:6–7

When you consider how Jesus healed people throughout his ministry, notice how differently he approached each one. There was no prescriptive answer for how to heal a person. There was no formula to follow. He did what he saw the Father doing. He did not hesitate even when it may have seemed foolish or unnecessary to the onlooker.

This blind man had probably heard many people spit in his direction as a sign of disgust for the curse they thought had brought about his blindness. In this case, when he heard Jesus spit on the ground, it was for his healing. There may be times when you feel led by the Spirit to do something that seems a little strange to your mind. If it does not cause harm and if it involves someone else's participation and they are open to it, then allow yourself to take a step of obedient faith.

*Healer, thank you for your creativity in meeting us. Open my eyes to your creativity in my own life.*

# Greater than Tradition

The people marched him over to the Pharisees to speak with them. They were concerned because the miracle Jesus performed by making clay with his saliva and anointing the man's eyes happened on a Sabbath day, a day that no one was allowed to "work."

JOHN 9:13–14

This is not the first time Jesus had performed a miracle on the Sabbath. Yet it was not something that the Pharisees could easily get over. The fact of the matter is that God is more concerned with people's well-being than he is with tradition. It is reminiscent of God's words in Hosea 6:6: "I want you to show love, not offer sacrifices. I want you to know me more than I want burnt offerings" (NLT).

As humans, we are creatures of habit. Traditions make us feel safe and comfortable because we know what to expect. However, God is always doing something new. The earth and our lives are cyclical, not lived out on a straight and linear path. As followers of Christ, we must value God's nature more than we do our own comfort. How can we take steps in that direction today?

*Christ, thank you for being so persistent in mercy that you did not allow the traditions of people to keep you from healing those in need. Help me to reprioritize my own values, not putting my own schedule ahead of the needs of others.*

# Stubborn Hearts

Still refusing to believe that the man had been healed and was truly blind from birth, the Jewish leaders called for the man's parents to be brought to them.

JOHN 9:18

There were people who missed out on the joy of the blind man's healing because they were so caught up in stubbornness. They refused to recognize the wonder of what happened. Even bringing in the parents of the man, they were full of harsh skepticism.

It was not curiosity that drove the Jewish leaders to find the blind man's parents and hear their story. They wanted to disprove Jesus. They were driven by a vendetta against him, and many of them would not budge at all, let alone concede that Jesus was who he said he was. This is a good example of how bias can drive us to great lengths to avoid reality. Instead of being like these stubborn men, may we choose to leave the door open to possibility, wonder, and, above all, God's goodness.

*Lord Jesus, will you unveil mindsets that have kept me from seeing the truth of who you are? Instead of having a stubborn heart, I want to have an open one.*

## Resisting Intimidation

(Now the parents were obviously intimidated by the Jewish religious leaders, for they had already announced to the people that if anyone publicly confessed Jesus as the Messiah, they would be excommunicated. That's why they told them, "Ask him, he's a mature adult. He can speak for himself.")

JOHN 9:22–23

The parents of the blind man refused to lie about their son's condition, but the religious leaders still intimidated them. The blind man's parents directed the leaders back to their son to answer for himself who he thought Jesus was. There was a lot at stake for them. Excommunication from the temple was no small thing. It is important to note that the reaction of the blind man's parents did not dishonor God.

Has being honest ever cost you something? Perhaps refusing to compromise your values or integrity has had a direct effect on your job, reputation, or life. Those in power may try to intimidate you so you bend to their will. Still, it is more important to know that you are being consistent and true, whatever that may look like in your circumstance.

*Jesus, when others try to intimidate me into compromising the truth, help me to stand strong and refuse to give in. I lean on your help.*

# No Longer Blind

The healed man replied, "I have no idea what kind of man he is. All I know is that I was blind and now I can see for the first time in my life!"

JOHN 9:25

At the point of this inquiry, the formerly blind man did not know who Jesus was. He only knew that before Jesus healed him, he had never seen a day in his life. After his miraculous encounter with the Christ, he had full vision. What a beautiful and merciful thing! Not only did Jesus offer this man physical sight, but he offers spiritual sight to all who dare to believe in him.

Perhaps you remember a time when you were blind to certain things in your life. Maybe you remember being caught in a cloud of confusion, and after an encounter with Christ, you could suddenly think clearly. Maybe you feel this way today. Whatever the case may be, all it takes is a moment with the Lord for something that was once a hindrance to become a pillar in your testimony. He offers freedom, clarity, and wisdom. Will you receive from him?

*God, thank you for the power of your mercy that still miraculously opens blind eyes and offers spiritual sight. Meet with me today and move in power.*

# True Faith

"We know that God doesn't listen to sinners, but only to godly people who do his will…I tell you, if this man isn't from God, he wouldn't be able to heal me like he has!"

JOHN 9:31, 33

When we encounter the power of God's kindness in our lives, it is undeniable. The healing that the blind man experienced made a difference in his ability to believe in Jesus as God. Think over when you first came to faith in Christ. What made the difference for you?

The testimony of our encounters with God is ours to share. These experiences are ours to remember and hold dear. They are the pillars of our personal faith. It is important to take time to think through what God has done for us, how he has met us with mercy, and how our lives transformed in response. As we remember, perhaps we will feel led to share it with someone else. As we do, we will find our own faith growing in remembrance, and our gratitude will lead us back to worship him yet again.

*Faithful God, there is nothing you cannot do. Remind me of the power of your love in my life and the way my heart has expanded in response. I believe that you are still working.*

# Heart of Grateful Devotion

The man whose blind eyes were healed answered, "Who is he, Master? Tell me so that I can place all my faith in him." Jesus replied, "You're looking right at him. He's speaking with you. It's me, the one in front of you now." Then the man threw himself at his feet and worshiped Jesus and said, "Lord, I believe in you!"

JOHN 9:36–38

The powerful mercy of God can transform our whole lives in a moment. When we are in need and God provides, when we are sick and we become well, or when we are in despair and find hope—these are all examples of how God can turn our lives around. In any wonderful, life-changing experience, gratitude cannot help but bubble up from within.

The blind man could now see. He knew that Jesus had done it and that Jesus' power completely transformed not only the blind man's present but also his future. His response was to put his complete faith in Jesus and worship him with grateful devotion. Let's take time to worship the One who meets us with the same powerful kindness today.

*Merciful Christ, your compassion shines through everything you do. Thank you for the ways you have met me already with kindness. Open my eyes in this moment to the truth and beauty of who you are. I worship you.*

## *Blinded by Pride*

Jesus said, "I have come to judge those who think they see and make them blind. And for those who are blind, I have come to make them see."

JOHN 9:39

God's glory shines brightest in our surrendered weakness. He judges those who think they have it all figured out. They refuse to admit their shortcomings, and they suffer for it. Jesus does not condemn what religion often does condemn. He was harshest with those who were full of pride. He was gentle with those the world scorned. He was merciful to those whom the religious order cast aside. He still is.

We must be diligent about surrendering our mindsets to the Lord. Where pride keeps us from growing, humility opens the door to understanding. Jesus came to open the eyes of the blind, spiritually as well as physically. He came to set the sinner free. He came to give us a spiritually rich and satisfying life. Let's lay aside our pride and receive what he so willingly offers.

*Miracle Maker, thank you for being patient with me. I humble myself before you. Where pride has kept me shut off from your mercy, I welcome your Spirit to work in me today.*

# Trustworthy and True

Jesus said to the Pharisees, "Listen to this eternal truth: The person who sneaks over the wall to enter into the sheep pen, rather than coming through the gate, reveals himself as a thief coming to steal."

JOHN 10:1

When people enter through the main door, they have nothing to hide. When they try to sneak in undetected, they clearly have ulterior motives. Thieves seek to claim what is not theirs. In the case of the example Jesus gives, the thief not only comes to steal what does not belong to him but is like a wolf that seeks to destroy what it finds.

Think of the most trustworthy people in your life. Who are the ones who refuse to dishonor, lie, or deceive? These are probably the people you feel safe being yourself with and those you can trust not to share your business with others. Don't waste your time trying to impress those who don't have the values of Christ's kingdom. Don't let their opinions be greater than God's. Look to the ones who are trustworthy and true, for they are safe places in a harsh world.

*Good Shepherd, give me discernment to know those to whom I should stop allowing access to my vulnerability and those whom I can trust. Thank you for wisdom that is grounded in your truth.*

## True Shepherd

"The true Shepherd walks right up to the gate, and because the gatekeeper knows who he is, he opens the gate to let him in. And the sheep recognize the voice of the true Shepherd, for he calls his own by name and leads them out, for they belong to him."

JOHN 10:2–3

God calls every sheep in his flock by name. If you look to the Lord, you can count on his leadership. If you belong to him, nothing in this world can keep him from finding you. He knows you by name, calls you out, and leads you into pastures of nourishment. He will never leave you alone to find your own way.

When was the last time you felt seen by the Lord? Think back to when you felt his gaze upon you, reading the depths of your heart and meeting you as you were. His kindness is palpable in his presence. Ask him to visit your fields today, to meet you in the pasture of your life, and to show you where he wants to lead you. There is confidence in knowing his leadership always operates out of love. Follow him, for he is trustworthy, and you belong to him.

*Shepherd, I will follow where you lead me today.*

# Knowing His Voice

"When he has brought out all his sheep, he walks ahead of them
and they will follow him, for they are familiar with his voice."

JOHN 10:4

Look to the true Shepherd today. Listen for his voice.
Those who belong to him know what he sounds like.
How? Because they learn his character, the timbre and tone
of his kind voice that calls out to his children. Ask him to
speak to you. If the fruit of the Spirit is present, then you
know that it is the Lord speaking. Where there is peace,
space to breathe, expansive love and understanding, where
there is joy, there is God with you.

The more time you spend with someone, the more easily
you can identify them. Most of us could probably pick out
our loved ones in a crowd. But an acquaintance we've only
met a couple times? Likely not. If you want to grow in confidence in knowing the Lord, the only way to do it is to spend
more time with him. As you do, you will learn to recognize
him even in the busiest moments of your day. Listen for his
voice and follow it today.

*Father, speak to me, for I am listening. I give you my time and
my attention.*

## Able to Discern

> "[My sheep] will run away from strangers and never follow them because they know it's the voice of a stranger."
>
> JOHN 10:5

We teach our children to not follow strangers. We teach them, in case they are separated from us, how to spot the difference between safe people—those whom they can likely trust—and those whom they should avoid. In the same way, certain signs help us discern those who may try to lead us away from our good Father.

The Holy Spirit is in us and with us to help us recognize the difference between leaders we can trust and those who are full of their own agendas. We owe our full allegiance to no one but the Lord. Anyone who requires us to blindly follow them based on their own word isn't a person we should entertain. There is so much rich wisdom in the Word of God to help us. Look at the Proverbs. Memorize the fruit of the Spirit in Galatians 5. Where the Spirit of the Lord is, there is freedom. Trust the intuition of wisdom and the caution of those who have your best at heart.

*Spirit, thank you for your discernment. I look to you, and I rely on your embodied wisdom to guide me away from danger.*

# The Gateway

"I am the Gateway. To enter through me is to experience life, freedom, and satisfaction."

JOHN 10:9

As our gatekeeper, Jesus remains with his flock and keeps them living in peace and safety. His voice, through his teachings, guards us against unreliable teachers who want to steal our hearts for their own. Only Jesus is our kind Shepherd, worthy of our affection.

When we enter through Christ, we experience life, freedom, and satisfaction. If this feels rote to us, then we need a fresh encounter with his presence. In him, we live and function and have our identity (see Acts 17:28). As Acts 17:27 says, "He is the God who is easy to discover!" This easy-to-discover God washes over us with the freedom of his mercy, the satisfaction our souls are longing for, and the abundance of his life within us. God promises us, "Even when [our] paths wind through the dark valley of tears…He gives to [us] a brook of blessing filled from the rain of an outpouring" (Psalm 84:6). What a beautiful and hopeful promise we can grab hold of right here and now, in this very moment.

*Gateway, I come through you to the place of my rest. You are my place of safety, and you bring refreshment to the deepest, weariest parts of my soul. Thank you.*

## Better than Expected

"A thief has only one thing in mind—he wants to steal, slaughter, and destroy. But I have come to give you everything in abundance, more than you expect—life in its fullness until you overflow!"

JOHN 10:10

Though the world is full of pain and suffering, the kingdom of Christ is full of peace. We cannot escape the painful trials of this life, but we can find our rest in the presence of God. He offers us more than we could ever expect. His life pours into our inner beings by his Spirit until we overflow his expansive love to all around us.

If the God you know is not better than your expectations, you have much more to experience of him. He never runs out of mercy to offer you. His peace never runs out. His presence is full of creative inspiration. He truly is better than you can ever imagine, so dare to see in him all the abundance that you are looking for and more. He alone can satisfy the depths of your longings.

*Glorious Lord, I trust that there is more goodness in you than I have yet encountered. I want to be awed by your kindness today. I receive from your abundance.*

# Good Shepherd

"I am the Good Shepherd who lays down my life
as a sacrifice for the sheep."

JOHN 10:11

A good shepherd does not run away from the threat of an enemy. He fights to protect his flock. In the end, if it costs him his life, he chooses to offer it for them. David was a shepherd boy. He fought off a bear and lion, stepping into harm's way in order to protect the sheep in his care.

Jesus went even further, laying down his life for all who would ever find refuge in his care. He offered it willingly. If he is our good Shepherd, then we are the flock grazing in his pasture. Though it may have seemed as if death had defeated Christ, we know that he conquered death when he rose again. Jesus arose triumphant from the grave, and he stands in that victory today. He is the good Shepherd who willingly sacrificed his life for his sheep, and he is alive and well, watching over us even now.

*Good Shepherd, thank you for being willing to lay down your life in our place. You are so wonderful. Thank you, too, that you are alive and still watching over us.*

## Truly Invested

> "The worker who serves only for wages is not a real shepherd. Because he has no heart for the sheep he will run away and abandon them when he sees the wolf coming. And then the wolf mauls the sheep, drags them off, and scatters them."
>
> JOHN 10:12–13

We never need to second-guess Jesus' motives toward us. He will never abandon us in our trouble because he loves us more than we can imagine. He laid down his very life for all. No one is excluded from his mercy-kindness. However used you have felt in the past—in any relationship—God is different. He provides everything we need to be free.

He is love, and in him we find ourselves completely and wholly accepted. He washes over us with the purity of his purposes, removing the weight of our endless expectation to produce results from our own efforts. He is invested in us every step of the way. He gives us strength to move through our suffering. He offers us the protection of his peace in the face of ravaging wolves. He is with us, and he will never leave us.

*Lord God, thank you for never running away from me or the troubles I face. I trust that you are with me in each and every one because you love me and are invested in my life.*

# Do You Recognize Him?

"I alone am the Good Shepherd,
and I know those whose hearts are mine,
for they recognize me and know me."

JOHN 10:14

We can rest in the knowledge that Christ sees our hearts. He knows what we don't even know how to verbalize. He sees through the facades we put up, and he reads our intentions, our desires, and our plans. He knows us so very well. What a comfort!

There is no doubt that Jesus can, at any moment, identify the hearts that belong to him. He says that those who recognize and know him are his, just as a flock recognizes the voice of their shepherd. He is their safe space and trusted protector. He is their guide and their keeper. How well do you recognize the voice of the Lord in your life? You do not have to hear a thing with your physical ears to acknowledge him. He speaks through nature, other people, his Word, and by his Spirit within you through impressions, wisdom, and truth. There are so many ways to spot him in your life. May you find that your awareness grows as you look to him more and more.

*Good Shepherd, thank you for knowing my heart. There is nothing to hide. I humble myself before you and ask for you to speak to me however you want to. I am listening; I am looking; I am open.*

## Sacrificial Love

"Just as my Father knows my heart and I know my Father's heart.
I am ready to give my life for the sheep."

JOHN 10:15

Jesus displayed to us the great love of God by laying down his life for us. As he said in John 15:13, "The greatest love of all is a love that sacrifices all. And this great love is demonstrated when a person sacrifices his life for his friends."

Have you ever sacrificed a part of your life for someone else? Perhaps you made the decision to change jobs to spend more time with your family. Maybe you decided to become a foster parent, opening your home to care for children in need. There are many ways that we can display sacrifice in our lives. In every way, it is our choice. If we don't feel we have a choice, then we are missing out on the agency offered to us through God. Even Jesus, knowing what he would face in coming to earth, *chose* to do it. Let's look for how we have been living with resentment and, instead, see where we can assert ourselves in love and choose which sacrifices we are willing to make.

*Christ Jesus, thank you for counting the cost of what it would mean for you to come to earth and for still making the choice. Open my eyes to where I have felt powerless so I can take ownership of my choices.*

# Shepherd of All

> "I have other sheep that I will gather which are not of this Jewish flock. And I, their shepherd, must lead them too, and they will follow me and listen to my voice. And I will join them all into one flock with one shepherd."
>
> JOHN 10:16

There is no one in this world whom Jesus does not love fully and completely. He wants everyone to look to him and be saved. "Turn your heart to me, face me now, and be saved wherever you are, even from the ends of the earth," God says in Isaiah 45:22. First Timothy 2:4 puts it even more succinctly: "He longs for everyone to embrace his life and return to the full knowledge of the truth." Though not everyone will choose to do it, the invitation goes out to all.

In this world, we like to congregate in groups where we feel safe, seen, and accepted. We all want to feel as if we belong somewhere. The love of God does not exclude anyone, so let's be sure that with our faith we are not building walls but bridges. The Shepherd of All will gather his people from every tribe, nation, people group, and language. As we wait for that day, let's open our hearts and our homes in loving hospitality to others.

*Jesus, you are the King over all. I will not withhold my kindness from people, no matter their differing background.*

# Willing Surrender

"I surrender my own life, and no one has the power to take my life from me. I have the authority to lay it down and the power to take it back again. This is the destiny my Father has set before me."

JOHN 10:18

It was probably important for the disciples to hear Jesus talk about offering his own life. They did not anticipate what was about to come, no matter how many times Jesus warned them. Still, in hindsight, they remembered all that he had said. Jesus knew what he was doing. It was no accident that led him to the cross.

It is much easier to blame others for our suffering than it is to take ownership of our choices. Everything has a risk. In every relationship, every job, there is always the potential that we may be rejected, hurt, or worse. Though we cannot see the future, we can assess at every step what we are willing to do. Jesus did, and so can we. When we love someone or something enough, we are willing to surrender our own comfort for them. May we recognize where we have a choice and let go of the impulse to blame others.

*Jesus, I am in awe that you willingly surrendered your life for me. You knew what was coming, and still you chose sacrifice. Thank you!*

# Seeds of Faith

> Then there were others who weren't so sure: "His teaching is full of insight. These are not the ravings of a madman! How could a demonized man give sight to one born blind?"
>
> JOHN 10:21

Not every religious leader was hard-hearted against Jesus. Some had the seeds of faith in their hearts, truly recognizing the wonder of Jesus' ministry. Who else, they figured, could give sight to a blind man? Jesus' teachings, they noted, were insightful and wise, not a lunatic's gibberish.

There may be times when we find ourselves in the minority in the way we think. That doesn't mean that we're wrong. We should be willing to recognize wisdom, no matter the package it comes in. As we continue to grow stronger in the values of God through fellowship with him, the easier it will be to spot those values out in the wild of things. Our hearts will become ready soil for seeds of faith to grow as we continue to submit to the wonder and ways of Christ.

*Jesus, may I always be open to your wisdom no matter where it is found. I trust that the foundation of your mercy, the guidance of the Spirit, and the teachings and revelations of the Father's heart will give me discernment. I believe in you, Anointed One.*

## Never Enough

> The Jewish leaders…said, "How much longer will you keep us in suspense? Tell us the truth and clarify this for us once and for all. Are you really the Messiah, the Anointed One?"
>
> JOHN 10:24

The Pharisees were not satisfied with any of the answers Jesus gave them as to his identity. Their offense and doubt kept their hearts clouded. They just wanted a reason to arrest Jesus. They did not ask because they truly wanted to know. If that had been the case, they would have already believed that Jesus was anointed.

Have you ever felt like someone was uninterested in knowing the truth about you? Perhaps they were bent on misunderstanding or underestimating you. Perhaps they just did not like you. It is not your job to make everyone around you happy, nor is it your responsibility to convince people of your worth. Some people are not interested in changing their minds. In this case, we have to let it go and keep being true to who we are. Even Jesus could not please everyone. He was not preoccupied with being liked, so we can also let go of that superficial goal. He was always loving and true. That is a much better ambition for us to have.

*Christ, you are enough, and I believe that I am too. I don't have to convince anyone to love or even like me. Help me to be true to who you say I am.*

## Miracle Proof

Jesus answered them, "I have told you the truth already and you did not believe me. The proof of who I am is revealed by all the miracles that I do in the name of my Father."

JOHN 10:25

J esus did not require that anyone just take him at his word. He moved in miraculous acts of mercy, healing bodies, feeding crowds with crumbs, and turning water into wine. He did all of this to prove his authority as God's Son. Everything he did was an act of goodness and generosity. Even when the Pharisees criticized him for it, they could find no real fault in his ministry.

It is okay to need more than someone's word to trust them. Actions reveal a person's character. If they are reliable, we will see it over time. If they are honest, there will be no hidden shame or lie to get caught up in. How they treat others will reflect their inner values. Let time reveal who they are, as well as how you feel when you are around them. It may not be miracle proof, but it will be proof, nonetheless.

*Lord, may I refuse to keep a closed mind to others. Help me to be patient and discerning, acting always in love.*

# Fruit of Mercy

Jesus said, "My Father has empowered me to work many miracles and acts of mercy among you. So which one of them do you want to stone me for?"

JOHN 10:32

The reaction of the Jewish leaders was clear. They did not plan on stoning Jesus because of anything good he did but because they could not handle him equating himself with God. Jesus himself addressed this in Matthew 7. He said that we are able to spot phony prophets by their actions and the fruits of their character. "You'll know them by the obvious fruit of their lives and ministries" (Matthew 7:20), and then you'll know whether they are true or false.

How many of us have overlooked the good works that others have done only to be angry at the confidence that they lived out? Jesus gave us clear directions to look at the fruit of a person's life. How each of us lives matters more than what we say we believe. Let's keep doing good, then, and letting the fruit of the Spirit speak for itself.

*Merciful One, keep me from being clouded by arrogance, and instead, may I see the clear fruit of the lives around me as the evidence of lives well-lived or untrustworthy persons. May the fruit of my life bring you honor.*

# Beautiful Works of God

"If you see me doing the beautiful works of God upon the earth, then you should at least believe the evidence of the miracles, even if you don't believe my words! Then you would come to experience me and be convinced that I am in the Father and the Father is in me."

JOHN 10:38

There are some mysteries that are undeniable when we encounter them. We cannot explain away the glory of a sunset, nor can we reason out the pictures we see of the edge of our universe. Many miracles are still happening in and around us. We have countless reasons to stop in awe for a breathless moment.

Jesus wants us to experience him. He wants us not only to believe but also to be convinced that he is in the Father and the Father is in him. When we catch glimpses of his merciful fingerprints in the world, if we would stop and acknowledge them, perhaps we would find ourselves face-to-face with the King of glory himself. There are so many beautiful works of God still happening in the world. May we have eyes to see and ears to hear what the Spirit is doing.

*Glorious God, I have already seen hints of your grandeur, and oh, how they have caused wonder to bubble up in me. Reveal yourself even more, Lord.*

# Prophetic Predictions

Many came out to where he was and said about him, "Even though John didn't perform any miracles, everything he predicted about this man is true!" And many people became followers of Jesus at the Jordan and believed in him.

JOHN 10:41–42

When prophecies become reality, peoples' faith will soar. Perhaps among some of the people who became followers of Jesus, they had a hesitation in their hearts until they realized that all that John had predicted about Jesus was true. These people knew John, and now they knew Jesus.

The patience of God permits a bit of skepticism. Jesus did not refuse those who had not followed him sooner. This was not the first time the people had seen Jesus. This was the very place where John had baptized him! Yet Jesus welcomed those who followed him, whether young, old, following for very long, or a new believer. He still welcomes them today. All the promises of God, every prophecy made about him, will come to pass. It's only a matter of time.

*Jesus, thank you for your incredible patience with me. Thank you for not rushing or coercing me but patiently showing up for me, nonetheless. I love you.*

## Authentic Request

> [Lazarus'] sisters sent a message to Jesus,
> "Lord, our brother Lazarus, the one you love,
> is very sick. Please come!"
>
> JOHN 11:3

When Martha and Mary of Bethany sent a request to Jesus to come to visit, it was because their brother was very sick. They longed for Jesus' presence, for they knew he would be able to heal Lazarus. "Please come!" they said. When a loved one is sick, don't we make the same entreaties to both family and God? "Come, be with them. Come, be with us." Only do come!

Jesus was close with this family. He loved them very much. As soon as he heard that Lazarus was sick, he planned to go. Whom would you want close to you in a time of crisis? Those you beckon to come are the ones who mean the most to you. Take some time today and reach out to them, letting them know how much you love and appreciate them. Call, send a note, or plan to meet up with them. Whatever you do, be grateful for the closeness of a friendship that reflects Jesus' love.

*Lord, I cannot forget to call to you. Come, Lord. Come to me in my need and in my sorrow, in my peace and in my joy. Please come!*

## Promises of Glory

When he heard this, he said, "This sickness will not end in death for Lazarus, but will bring glory and praise to God. This will reveal the greatness of the Son of God by what takes place."

JOHN 11:4

Jesus promised that the sickness of Lazarus would not end in death. Yet this promise was tested only a little while later. Does this mean Jesus was unaware of what was going to happen? No. He knew that if Lazarus died, he would raise Lazarus up again by the resurrection power of God.

There is often a space between promise and fulfillment where our expectations take a hit. When they do, will we change our views of God, or will we trust him to do what he promised? As 2 Corinthians 1:20 says, "All of God's promises find their 'yes' of fulfillment in him." Christ is the fulfillment of every one of God's promises. He has all the glory and power, and he is oh so worthy. Let's put our trust in him, even when everything else is seemingly failing. He never will.

*King of Glory, your promises never return to you void. I believe you will do what you say you will do, and I believe even more that your nature will never change. I trust you.*

*It's Time*

Even though Jesus loved Mary, Martha, and Lazarus, he remained where he was for two more days. Finally, on the third day, he said to his disciples, "Come. It's time to go to Bethany."

JOHN 11:5–7

Jesus did not rush to Bethany. He took two more days before he went. We look at this through the lens of history, knowing it all came together just fine. Imagine what it must have felt like for Mary and Martha, though, as the days ticked by, and Jesus still didn't show up.

We can trust God's timing, even when we don't understand it. Jesus is never late. He is not pushed or pulled by our priorities. All things are possible to him, so he needn't rush in anxiety. We don't know the reason why Jesus waited those two days before going to Bethany, but we do know he was faithful to fulfill his promise. We know that his love never diminished. When it was the right time, he went. If you find yourself in the space of waiting, trust. He will come. He is faithful. He is on time.

*Jesus, I trust your timing more than I trust my own anxiety. You are not moved by fear. Fill me with the peace of your presence as I wait.*

# *Walk in the Light*

Jesus replied, "Are there not twelve hours of daylight in every day?
You can go through a day without the fear of stumbling when you
walk in the One who gives light to the world. But you will stumble
when the light is not in you, for you'll be walking in the dark."

JOHN 11:9–10

When you walk in the light of day, there is no reason to fear what lies hidden in shadows. You don't fear stumbling over obstacles when you can see them clearly. Jesus is the one who gives light to the world. When we move in him, he lights up our path. We can avoid the obstructions by simply walking around them.

Jesus is the Word of God, as the beginning of the book of John revealed. He is the Way, the Truth, and the Light. Psalm 119:105 says this: "Truth's shining light guides me in my choices and decisions; the revelation of your Word makes my pathway clear." Jesus guides us in our choices and decisions. The light of who he is makes our pathway clear. Why, then, would we ever try to walk alone?

*Light of God, you are the one I look to for direction and discernment. Light the path before me as I walk with you.*

# Time for Awakening

Jesus added, "Lazarus, our friend, has just fallen asleep.
It's time that I go and awaken him."

JOHN 11:11

In the moment that Lazarus died, Jesus knew it. Though the people around him didn't understand exactly what Jesus was saying at the time, Jesus was getting ready to raise Lazarus from the dead.

There are times in our lives when what we love dearly goes dormant. Some remain in that sleeping state for the rest of our lives, while others are meant to be reawakened. Spend some time in the presence of God, asking him if any areas are ready to be awakened. He is faithful to resurrect old dreams when their time has come. Dare to believe that what God is stirring within you is ready for its resurrection. Follow his lead and go to the tomb with the Resurrection and the Life, ready for what he will do.

*Christ, you bring life to the dead, and they are new again. I trust you to do this in my life. Awaken me in your presence, Lord, for I want to walk in the light of day with you. Show me where you want to move, and I will follow you.*

# Opportunity to Trust

Jesus made it plain to them, "Lazarus is dead. And for your sake, I'm glad I wasn't there, because now you have another opportunity to see who I am so that you will learn to trust in me. Come, let's go and see him."

JOHN 11:14–15

Speaking clearly to his disciples, Jesus laid out what he was going to do. This was another opportunity for his disciples to see who he was, working in miracle power. They had witnessed him heal the lame, feed thousands, as well as perform other miracles. They had not, however, watched him call a dead man out of his crypt. This miracle would go far in teaching the disciples to trust Jesus as the Son of God even more.

When faced with challenges that seem insurmountable in our lives, they are opportunities for us to trust God. We get to grow in trusting his character through it all. He is who he says he is. We get to grow in our wonder of his mercy and power. He really is with us. He really is for us. He will work out what we cannot possibly do on our own. Let's trust him to do it and cast our worries aside.

*Messiah, I believe that you can do anything, even raise a decomposing body back to life again. I trust you with the challenges in my life, Lord. Do what only you can do!*

*July*

# Difference in Perspective

Thomas, nicknamed the Twin, remarked to the other disciples,
"Let's go so that we can die with him."

JOHN 11:16

In returning to Judea, Jesus and his disciples were taking a great risk. The Jewish leaders had nearly stoned Jesus just a short time before. Thomas, thinking through this risk, figured it was a death sentence to return to the region. Even though this was a pessimistic way of thinking, he was still willing to go. If it would cost their lives, Thomas figured, they might as well still follow Jesus.

We can be quick to judge others' perspectives when they are not the same as our own. If we like to look on the bright side, a cynic can certainly get on our nerves. If we consider ourselves practical people, those who seem to have their heads in the clouds may frustrate us. In any case, no matter what the differences in our perspectives, we can still choose to show up for each other. Looking at things differently does not automatically mean that we won't choose the same things in the end.

*Lord, you made us all so differently. Help me to keep myself from judging others' personalities when they still show the important values of your kingdom. Thank you!*

# Deep in Grief

When they arrived at Bethany, which was only about two miles from Jerusalem, Jesus found that Lazarus had already been in the tomb for four days.

JOHN 11:17–18

In the eyes of the mourners, when Jesus and his disciples arrived at Bethany, they were four days late. Lazarus had already been buried. They had done all that needed to be done. They had wrapped him in grave clothes, placed him in the crypt, and begun their mourning. Jesus was too late. At least, that is what they might have felt.

We know that Jesus was not, in fact, too late. He is the Son of God, who raises the dead to life with resurrection power. Still, he did not rush in and go straight to the grave of his friend and call him out. First, he met with his family. He met them in their mourning, even sharing the sorrow with them. Jesus also meets us in our grief. When all feels lost and as if time has stolen what we dearly loved, let's look for where Jesus encounters us. He is ever so loving and kind, and his presence is a balm to our heartbreak.

*Jesus, I'm so glad that you don't reprimand me for my grief. No, instead, you grieve with me. You're so gracious, kind, and faithful.*

## A Chance for Faith

Martha said to Jesus, "My Lord, if only you had come sooner, my brother wouldn't have died. But I know that if you were to ask God for anything, he would do it for you." Jesus told her, "Your brother will rise and live."

JOHN 11:21–23

In the face of Jesus, Martha lamented, "If only you had come sooner, my brother wouldn't have died." She did not end her thought there, however. She went on to say, "But I know that if you were to ask God…he would do it for you." In other words, she was leaving an opening for Jesus to surprise her. This may not have even been her intention, but it was a seed of faith, nonetheless.

Have you ever been met by disappointment, recognizing that "if only" something or other had happened, things would be okay? Jesus did not fail Martha, Mary, or Lazarus, even when it might have seemed to them as if he had. Jesus promised that Lazarus would rise and live. His promise to you may be different, but listen for his voice. Listen for his promise. He can turn your disappointment into a reason to celebrate.

*Loving Lord, when I can't reconcile my circumstances with your nature, speak your words of life to me. I need to know that you are still with me.*

# Resurrection Life

"Martha," Jesus said, "You don't have to wait until then.
I am the Resurrection, and I am Life Eternal.
Anyone who clings to me in faith, even though he dies,
will live forever."

JOHN 11:25

Jesus is Life Eternal. Jesus promised that when we cling to him in faith, we will dwell eternally with him. This is a spiritual hope, one that transcends time and space. It reaches into the distant future and somehow still is as pertinent today. When Jesus declared this to Martha, he had just told her that Lazarus would rise and live. Though Martha believed this for the future, she did not realize that Jesus was giving her hope for today.

Have you ever encountered the resurrection life of Jesus? Have you witnessed the power of God breaking through your expectation to a glorious new reality? The mercy of God is palpable. Yes, there are times when God causes us to wait. There are some prayers that don't get answered the way we expect. Yet there is Jesus, all the same, the Resurrection and the Life. He breathes into dreams long since buried and gives them new life. He offers us restoration in ways that seem too good to be true. We have only to trust him.

*God of Eternity, I cannot begin to understand the way you operate, but I am beginning to understand your mercy. Remind me that you are always with me, Lord, as I look to you.*

# The Power of Belief

"The one who lives by believing in me will never die.
Do you believe this?"

JOHN 11:26

Not only did Jesus come to restore life to his friend, Lazarus, but he also came to bring life to the whole world. This directs us back to what Jesus said in John 3:16, that "everyone who believes in him will never perish but experience everlasting life." Who gets to experience eternal life? Those who believe in Christ as the Son of God. And those who truly believe in him will live out his values on the earth.

We are so quick to push past the power of belief that Jesus spoke of. We look for the evidence and transformation, almost demanding it at once. Faith is a journey, though. It develops and refines over time. It is something to be practiced, to be formed as we walk it out. But first, faith is a gift. Anyone, no matter their abilities, their education, or class, can believe. It is a beautiful and powerful act of joining our will to the gift of God's grace. What a generous Savior we have!

*Anointed One, thank you for offering the same opportunity to everyone who comes to you. You are so generous in mercy. I believe in you!*

## For Us

Then Martha replied, "Yes, Lord, I do! I've always believed that you are the Anointed One, the Son of God who has come into the world for us!"

JOHN 11:27

The Anointed One came into the world *for us*. This means that God's heart is *for us*. He does not look for ways to condemn us but to draw us in with his kindness. He longs that all should know his powerful mercy. This love is triumphant! Romans 8:31 says this: "If God has determined to stand with us…who then could ever stand against us?" And later in verse 32, Paul added, "Since God freely offered [Christ] up as the sacrifice for us all, he certainly won't withhold from us anything else he has to give."

What more is there to say? If God is for us, who could come against us and win? This does not mean that we won't suffer in this life. It doesn't mean we get to escape pain. No, but Jesus Christ is triumphant over death and over the fear that reigns in darkness. He has come into the world for us, so our response to run to him is the right one.

*Lord, I believe that you are for your people and that your people are not an exclusive group. I believe that your love still moves you today. Move me in it as I surrender to you.*

## Loving Pursuit

She left and hurried off to her sister, Mary, and called her aside from all the mourners and whispered to her, "The Master is here and he's asking for you."

JOHN 11:28

Imagine someone whispering this in *your* ear: "The Master is here, and he's asking for you." Take some time to meditate on that experience. Let your ears perk up and feel the excitement and relief that Mary must have felt. He had come! He was here! And, on top of all of that, he was asking to see her.

Jesus is Immanuel, God with us. He is present in every situation you face. Let that really sink in. He lovingly pursues your heart. He is here, even now. Let your heart respond as it will. Spend some time with your Savior, communing spirit to Spirit. He is near. Turn to him and find consolation and peace in his presence.

*Immanuel, thank you for being so very near. I take the time to turn my attention to you. As I do, reveal how close you have been this whole time. I long for you, Jesus. Revive my weary heart in your powerful love again.*

## Run to Him

When Mary heard this,
she quickly went off to find him.

JOHN 11:29

W hat is your response to knowing God wants your attention? Is it to put it off for another time, or do you take the opportunity to run into his presence? This isn't a shame tactic—not at all! Jesus showed up in Bethany in response to Martha and Mary's request. He was later than they expected, but he was there. Mary could have hesitated, harboring a grudge against her Savior, but this is not what she did. She ran to find him.

It doesn't take us moving a muscle to turn our attention to Christ. All it takes is a turning of our minds and hearts. We can quickly go to find him even when we're commuting to work. We can run to him with our hearts wide open no matter where we are. Let's take the opportunity, then, to find him, for he wants to speak with us. He wants to meet with us, and we will find ourselves met with a warm embrace every time.

*Savior, I run to you with all that I am. When I'm walking the dog, drinking my coffee, or at work, you are accessible wherever I am. Thank you. Meet with me, Lord, as I turn to you over and over again throughout my day.*

*If Only*

When Mary finally found Jesus outside the village, she fell at his feet in tears and said, "Lord, if only you had been here, my brother would not have died."

JOHN 11:32

Martha and Mary both felt the sting of regret, even in the presence of Jesus. "If only you had been here." Think about the times when you have felt this way toward the Lord. Get really specific. If only you had been here, my dad wouldn't have died. If only you had been here, my marriage would have been saved. If only you had been here, [fill in the blank].

We don't have to hide our disappointment from Jesus. He already knows our hearts. We can take our pain and our if-onlys straight to Jesus. We get to express our feelings to the Lord without fear of shame, misunderstanding, or reprimand. Even though things have turned out differently than you expected, it does not mean that Christ has abandoned you. In fact, he promised that he never will. "I will never leave you, never! And I will not loosen my grip on your life" (Hebrews 13:5).

*Jesus, I love you! Thank you for allowing me—all of me—to show up before you consistently. You welcome me as I am, and for that, I am forever grateful.*

## *Moved with Tenderness*

When Jesus looked at Mary and saw her weeping at his feet, and all her friends who were with her grieving, he shuddered with emotion and was deeply moved with tenderness and compassion.

JOHN 11:33

Jesus Christ, both as a human being and as the one who came to show us what God the Father is like, had intense emotions. He felt sadness and pain. He feels your pain, and he is with you in your grief. All that he experienced during his time on earth is a gateway for us to relate to him. When Jesus saw Mary weeping at his feet, along with all her friends who grieved with her, he was overcome with emotion. He was deeply moved with tenderness and compassion.

When you grieve, this is what Jesus feels toward you. He is overcome with emotion against the realities that you are facing, and he is also filled with tenderness for you. His compassion toward you is like heat radiating from the sun. It reaches you. May you feel the warmth of his tenderness today even in your disappointments and heartbreak. He is moved for you. How deeply he cares for you!

*Compassionate One, thank you for the power of your love that meets me in my pain. Reach my soul with your tenderness today. I love you.*

# Deeply Feeling

Tears streamed down Jesus' face.

JOHN 11:35

There is a time to cry and a time to laugh, as the Scriptures say (see Ecclesiastes 3:4). Not only is this true of all humanity, but this was also true of Jesus. When Jesus wept at the grave of his friend, he already knew that he was going to bring Lazarus back to life. This did not stop Jesus from expressing his emotion. This is really important for us to note. When we want to push aside our feelings, the example of Jesus weeping at Lazarus' grave should give us space to grieve even while we continue trusting God's plan.

Emotion is not a bad thing. Being upset is not something we need to avoid. Our bodies need to process our feelings, and one of the ways they do that is to cry. Do you allow yourself to express your emotions when they build up within you, or do you try to reason yourself out of them? We were created in God's image, and we know that God weeps with those who weep. Let's stop shoving our emotions aside and instead allow ourselves to express them, whether we're with close friends or alone in our homes.

*Lord Jesus, thank you for not holding your tears back when you stood at the grave of Lazarus. Help me to allow the emotions I feel without needing to be defined by them.*

# Stones Rolled Away

Jesus, with intense emotions, came to the tomb—
a cave with a stone placed over its entrance.
Jesus told them, "Roll away the stone."

JOHN 11:38–39

When Jesus commanded that the stone be rolled away from Lazarus' tomb, Martha warned that her brother's body had already started decomposing. This was not something that Jesus overlooked. He knew what he was doing. Have you ever gone into a situation knowing that others would call you crazy, and it didn't matter? When you know that what you're doing is important, it doesn't matter what others say.

Perhaps you have been grieving a loss in your own life. Jesus wants to bring you hope and life even if you cannot see how such a thing is possible. His resurrection power can resurrect even the dreams that have begun to decompose. As Ephesians 3:20 encourages us, "He will achieve infinitely more than your greatest request, your most unbelievable dream, and exceed your wildest imagination!"

*Almighty God, I trust that you know what you're doing more than I do. Astound me with your goodness and bring new life to where I have experienced tremendous loss. Thank you.*

# Reminder: Just Believe

Jesus looked at her and said,
"Didn't I tell you that if you will believe in me,
you will see God unveil his power?"

JOHN 11:40

We all need reminders of God's faithfulness. Martha needed one in that moment, and Jesus graciously repeated to her his promise. In the space between promise and fulfillment, we may lose perspective, hope, or faith. Even in these cases, God is gracious with us. He reminds us of who he is, his unfailing faithfulness, and who we are to him.

If this meets you in a time of doubt, take it as an encouragement to remember what Christ said and did at first. Believe in him. Don't abandon the hope that he put in you. He has not changed. He is still loyal to his Word, loving toward his creation, and wonderfully powerful to do more than you can imagine. He will not let you down. Even if what you thought would be has passed away, allow him to revive your hopes in the reality of his perspective. His plans are better than any you could dream up on your own.

*Faithful One, I take time today to remember who you truly are. Remind my heart of your promises, your goodness, and your faithfulness. I believe in you.*

# Confidence in Prayer

They rolled away the heavy stone. Jesus gazed into heaven and said, "Father, thank you that you have heard my prayer, for you listen to every word I speak. Now, so that these who stand here with me will believe that you have sent me to the earth as your messenger, I will use the power you have given me."

JOHN 11:41–42

Not only is Jesus with us in our pain and grief, but he also takes action. Before his friend's grave, he shouted with authority, using the power that his heavenly Father had given him to make a remarkable difference in the situation. He did not come to destroy anything in God's name but to heal and bring life.

The confidence that Jesus had in his prayer is something that he offers us in relationship to God the Father through him. "So now we draw near freely and boldly to where grace is enthroned," Hebrews 4:16 says. We come boldly to the throne of grace, knowing that God hears our cries. The power of God brings life to those whom it touches. Come to God freely in prayer and be met with the power of Christ in your innermost being.

*Jesus, you reflected the power and love of the Father so well. What an honor it is to follow you! I love you.*

# Called out of the Grave

With a loud voice Jesus shouted with authority:
"Lazarus! Come out of the tomb!"

JOHN 11:43

We don't have to physically die to relate to Lazarus being called out of his tomb. Most of us can probably identify areas of our lives where we have felt dormant, stuck, or lifeless. Just as Jesus called out to his friend, he calls to those lifeless parts of us today. He does not leave us to rot away. He comes to us and calls out to us.

Will we heed his voice? Will we come out of our dark, stuffy spaces and into the light of his glorious presence? Jesus Christ has the authority to overcome death, and he certainly has the power to break us out of our captivity. He is our Defender, our Savior, and our reliable friend. When he calls us, what other response is there but to come running—or, in some cases, stumbling—toward him? He removes our grave clothes and liberates us.

*Liberator, there truly is no one like you. Speak to the parts of me that need resurrection and call them out. I am yours, and I come alive in you.*

# *Help to Unravel*

In front of everyone, Lazarus, who had died four days earlier,
slowly hobbled out—he still had grave clothes tightly wrapped
around his hands and feet and covering his face! Jesus said to
them, "Unwrap him and let him loose."

JOHN 11:44

When we first come out of a place where we were
dormant and bound up, it may be with slow, hob-
bling steps. As we walk out, the grave clothes that wrapped
up that part of us may still seem tightly bound. We will
need them to be unraveled. Jesus said to the people around
Lazarus, "Unwrap him and let him loose." We may also need
the devotion of friends to help us detangle old, limiting ideas
so that we may be free.

Think of a time when you relied on the care of friends
to help you through a transition. God created us for community. We are not meant to rely on our own strength all the
time to "power through." No, we all need help at different
times, and it is to our benefit to rely on each other.

*Lord, it is a beautiful thing that you involve us in each other's
freedom. May I not miss an opportunity to help my friends in
their times of need.*

## Personal Experience

From that day forward many of those who had come to visit Mary believed in him, for they had seen with their own eyes this amazing miracle!

JOHN 11:45

Though many of Mary's friends had most likely heard through her about how wonderful Jesus was, it was when they saw for themselves Jesus perform an amazing miracle that they believed in him. Personal experience made all the difference for them, and often it does for us too.

Think about someone in your life whom you had heard wonderful things about, but until you met that person for yourself, you felt indifferent toward him or her. How did that change when you got to know the person better? When we have no context or personal connection to a person, though their reputation may be wonderful, it does not affect us much. Jesus is accessible to all of us in the same measure, and he promises to reveal himself to those who seek him. Let's go after him for our own personal experience. There is nothing wrong with that motive, for the nature of God is unchanged either way.

*Lord Jesus, tasting and seeing your goodness changes everything. I believe that you are full of mercy, power, and truth. You are just. I believe in you.*

# Motivations Matter

The Pharisees and the chief priests called a special meeting of the High Council and said, "So what are we going to do about this man? Look at all the great miracles he's performing! If we allow him to continue like this, everyone will believe in him. And the Romans will take action and destroy both our country and our people!"

JOHN 11:47–48

The Jewish religious leaders could not deny how powerful Jesus was. They spoke of his great miracles, fearing that if they didn't stop him, then everyone would believe in him. If this happened, it would threaten their influence and authority. Though they had the inclination to protect their people, they more likely wanted to preserve their own comfort and places of power.

Our motivations can either guide us to the truth or away from it. In the case of many of the Pharisees, they saw the power of God moving through Jesus. Still, their self-preservation instincts kept them from embracing him. Admitting his truth would mean denying their own opinions and stances. This is why a humble heart is so important. We must be willing to admit when we are wrong so that we can receive the blessed truth.

*Lord, I choose to humble my heart today, admitting that there is so much I don't yet understand or know. Teach me and lead me to the truth.*

## One Big Sacrifice

"Don't you realize we'd be much better off if this one man were to die for the people than for the whole nation to perish?" (This prophecy that Jesus was destined to die for the Jewish people didn't come from Caiaphas himself, but he was moved by God to prophesy as the chief priest.)

JOHN 11:50–51

Jesus' sacrifice was for all people. God took even the wicked intentions of the lead priests of Jesus' day and turned them around to incorporate them into his plan. Take courage that God can do the same with any hard thing you are facing, no matter how unjust it is.

You are not alone in what you are going through. You don't have to rely on your waning strength to keep you afloat. No matter how terrible the things you are facing, Jesus has done everything to make you right with God. This is reason to rejoice! As Romans 4:25 reminds us, "Jesus was handed over to be crucified for the forgiveness of our sins and was raised back to life to prove that he had made us right with God!" In Christ, we are completely forgiven, free, and at peace with God.

*Savior, I believe that your powerful mercy covers everything. Even the hardest trials of my life are drenched in your love. With you, I will get through it. Thank you.*

# United as One

(Jesus' death would not be for the Jewish people only,
but to gather together God's children scattered
around the world and unite them as one.)

JOHN 11:52

Isaiah 49:6 states, "I will make you to be a light to the nations and to bring the light of my salvation to the ends of the earth!" We know that Jesus is the light to the nations. His sacrifice was to cover not only the Jewish nation but also every nation, tribe, and tongue. Under Christ, we are meant to be *united* by his love.

When we are overly concerned about our own comfort rather than the well-being of all people, we lose sight of God's compassion. The love of God reaches out, and it has no boundaries. It doesn't stay safe or stored up for a rainy day. There is always more than enough. There is grace to empower us to reach out to one another, to bear each other's burdens, and to invite more people to the communal table. May we unite under Christ and his love rather than distancing ourselves from one another.

*Jesus, you are the Savior of the whole world. There is not one person whom you don't cover in the power of your love—whether or not they receive it. May I see through your perspective rather than the biases and limitations of my own.*

# Seasons of Seclusion

> For this reason Jesus no longer went out in public among the Jews. But he went in the wilderness to a village called Ephraim, where he secluded himself with his disciples.
>
> JOHN 11:54

Under persecution from the Jewish leaders, Jesus went into a time of hiding. He went away with his closest friends, where he was safe and secluded. When the pressures of life get to be too much to bear, we can learn from Jesus' example. Sometimes hunkering down with our loved ones is the best thing we can do. Though seclusion is not what we are created to do forever, seasons of solitude can be extremely grounding and healing.

When was the last time you retreated from the world? Whether it was something you chose for yourself or something you felt driven to do in order to feel safe, the wilderness can be a place where we remember who we are. Jesus went into the wilderness on more than one occasion, so when we find ourselves in similar seasons, let's remember that it doesn't mean we have done anything wrong. Life is full of ups and downs, but God is faithfully with us through them all.

*Jesus, help me to find rest, refreshed perspective, and consolation in seasons of seclusion with my core friends and family. Spirit, be near and reveal how you are working.*

## Among Friends

Six days before the Passover began,
Jesus went back to Bethany,
the town where he raised Lazarus from the dead.

JOHN 12:1

Before Jesus went back to Jerusalem, he stopped at a place that was dear to his heart. In Bethany, Jesus found himself among close friends. These were people he loved and who loved him. It is a beautiful thing to be among those we love before embarking on a next big step. Jesus knew the importance of this.

We never need to apologize for checking in with loved ones when we need support. In fact, in the fellowship of close friends, we can rest as well as gain courage and strength for what lies ahead. If we need to be around those who believe in us, we are free to return to these places. Jesus returned to Bethany, where many believed in who he was. They welcomed and accepted him there. Though he knew he could not stay there forever, he embraced the opportunity to be among friends. Let's do the same whenever we need it.

*Jesus, the next time I feel I need to just push forward into the hard thing, bring to mind this example of you going back to Bethany. Thank you for the friends who are safe places of respite and encouragement to my soul.*

## Prepare a Feast

They had prepared a supper for Jesus. Martha served, and
Lazarus and Mary were among those at the table.

JOHN 12:2

When Jesus came to town, his friends set to work preparing a meal for him. They not only welcomed him but also served him. Think about a time when someone you love came to visit you. Did you expect them to fend for themselves, or did you host them? Now consider how you could do the same with the presence of Christ in your life.

You don't have to cook a meal in order to be hospitable to Jesus. You can prepare a dedicated time to spend with the Lord. You can offer a dedicated space in your home. We all have something to offer, and it is something that we don't have to go searching for. Looking at your day ahead, what do you have that you can offer to the Lord? What can you serve him?

*Lord Jesus, I offer you what I have today, and I make room for you in my schedule, in my attention, and in my physical spaces. I will continually turn my attention to you, remembering that you are with me. I want to host your presence well.*

# Extravagant Worship

Mary picked up an alabaster jar filled with nearly a liter of extremely rare and costly perfume—the purest extract of nard, and she anointed Jesus' feet. Then she wiped them dry with her long hair. And the fragrance of the costly oil filled the house.

JOHN 12:3

As Jesus sat at his friends' table, it is likely that his heart was heavy. He knew what was coming. His upcoming journey to Jerusalem signified the end of his earthly life. Perhaps Mary sensed this grief. She took out her best bottle of perfume, and, doing what can only be characterized as extravagant worship, she anointed his feet with the costly oil. She anointed him in the way that royal kings in Israel were anointed.

When we offer Christ the extravagance of our worship, he honors it. Nothing is too costly for him. He is worthy of it all. What a confirmation and encouragement Mary's act must have been to Jesus' heart! The fragrance was a physical reminder of his identity. What costly gift have you offered Jesus? An overflow of love leads us to offer him what may feel foolish to others. His reception is the only one that matters.

*Christ, I offer you my unrestrained worship today. You are worthy of my love, my sacrifice, and my life. Be glorified!*

## *Widen Your Scope*

"What a waste! We could have sold this perfume for a fortune
and given the money to the poor!"

JOHN 12:5

Judas' reaction may sound pious and practical, but it was clear that he did not understand the significance of Mary's offering. Whereas Jesus saw it as a beautiful sacrifice of love, Judas saw it as a waste of resources.

Perhaps you struggle with seeing things as wasted. Maybe you are preoccupied with the cost of things. When we look through the eyes of lack, we only see missed opportunities. When we look with the eyes of abundance, we realize that generosity is a beautiful act of love. When we can only criticize the actions of others, it is a clue that we need to realign our values and look with a wider scope. Let's seek to understand what drives other people. Let's lay down the pride in our own perceptions. Only then can we begin to perceive the magnitude of God's mercy.

*Loving Lord, I don't want to be so caught up in my understanding of things that I fail to see how you receive others. I want to learn from you, not build an argument on your behalf. I humble myself before you. Teach me, Lord.*

# Great Defender

Jesus said to Judas, "Leave her alone! She has saved it for the time of my burial. You'll always have the poor with you; but you won't always have me."

JOHN 12:7–8

J esus did not leave Judas' small-minded criticism unchecked. Rather, he called him on it. We do not have to worry about being misunderstood by Christ. He knows our hearts and intentions. He received Mary's act of love and defended her. Don't worry; he does the same for you. Even when others criticize you for what they perceive as reckless, unnecessary, or unacceptable actions, Jesus stands on your side. What you offer in love, he accepts.

May we be careful not to join in criticizing how others worship the Lord. It is not our business to manage or control them. What Jesus accepts, we had better not judge. When we focus more on how others are living than we do on our own lives—including our motivations, intentions, and attitudes— we miss out on opportunities to make a difference. Let's focus on what is ours to do and let Jesus defend us against the naysayers.

*Lord Jesus, thank you for being my defender. I will not let others' perceptions of me keep me from living for you. I love you!*

# What Kind of Plans

This prompted the chief priests to seal their plans to do away with both Jesus and Lazarus.

JOHN 12:10

When the chief priests heard that large crowds were going out to meet Jesus and Lazarus outside of Jerusalem, they took it as a threat to their own influence. Their plans reflected their hearts. They were not interested in the love of God that Jesus preached and exemplified. They wanted to preserve their places of power.

We must be aware of our motivations. Our motivations may drive us, but we can also humble our hearts and redirect as necessary. With awareness comes the opportunity for change. No matter what has driven you in the past, today you can choose whether this is how you want to continue to live. If those motivations don't represent what you actually want, take action today. It is never too late to change your mind, and the grace of God is there to help you to walk it out. Lean on the help of God, and you can redirect your energy.

*Lord, I don't want to be driven by self-protective ideals that keep me from walking in true freedom. I don't want to oppose your mercy, Lord. Transform me as I walk in your light.*

# Triumphant Entry

The next day the news that Jesus was on his way to Jerusalem swept through the massive crowd gathered for the feast. So they took palm branches and went out to meet him. Everyone was shouting, "Lord, be our Savior! Blessed is the one who comes to us sent from YAHWEH, the King of Israel!"

JOHN 12:12–13

Grabbing what was convenient, the people took palm branches to wave as Jesus entered Jerusalem. Even so, the palms represented something deeper. The palm tree is a symbol of victory over death, thriving in places where it must overcome arid climates. Jesus was likely reminded of his upcoming victory-over-death mission as he passed through the crowds of people waving palms in his direction.

Think about the ordinary objects you have around you. What could you use to praise the triumphant King? He walks into and through your life through his Spirit. Recognize his coming, his persistence, and his faithfulness as he draws near. Take what you have and praise him for all that he has done. He is ever so worthy.

*Triumphant King, you never cease to move in mercy, and your presence is as persistent today as it ever has been or will be. I worship you with all I have.*

# No Detail Overlooked

Jesus found a young donkey and rode on it to fulfill what was prophesied: "People of Zion, have no fear! Look—it's your king coming to you riding on a young donkey!"

JOHN 12:14–15

The conquering kings of Israel would ride on a warhorse or in a golden chariot, yet Jesus entered Jerusalem on a domesticated donkey. The true King of Israel is the King of Peace. What a wonderful Savior he is! Zechariah 9:9 prophesied that Zion's king would come humble, riding on a donkey. No prophecy was left unfulfilled.

Take courage today that God does not overlook a single detail of his promises. What he has said, he will do. What he has promised, he will fulfill. Certainly our understanding of how God works falls short, and we may need to adjust our specific expectations. Still, God's ways are more thorough than our own. He sees connections that we don't have the perspective to see. He is trustworthy, so let's throw our anchor of hope into the sea of his faithfulness.

*King of Kings, your ways are better than ways of the leaders of this world. You bring peace where others wage war. You offer freedom where others seek to hold us captive. You are the great Liberator and Savior. I trust you with my life.*

# Clarity of Hindsight

Jesus' disciples didn't fully understand the importance of what was taking place, but after he was raised and exalted into glory, they understood how Jesus fulfilled all the prophecies in the Scriptures that were written about him.

JOHN 12:16

As we're living our lives, we often fail to see the present moment clearly. We cannot take in all the information at once. Through the lens of hindsight, however, what was working together all along comes together in a much clearer picture. Even the disciples of Jesus did not understand the impact of all the details of Jesus' ministry. Yet, looking back, they understood how Jesus fulfilled the prophecies written about the Messiah.

Don't be discouraged if you don't understand the importance of this season of your life. God is with you through it all, and you will one day look back and see how he never left your side. If you find yourself in a time of grief, it may feel as dark as night, but know this: the sun will shine on you again, and you will see where the mercy of God has kept you. Not only this, but the seeds of your grief will bloom into gardens of glory.

*Lord, I hold on to you with all my might. I trust that you are working things together under the surface and that I will one day see it clearly.*

*Spread the News*

All the eyewitnesses of the miracle Jesus performed when he called Lazarus out of the tomb and raised him from the dead kept spreading the news about Jesus to everyone.

JOHN 12:17

Spread the news of what God has done in your life. What power have you witnessed with your own eyes? What loving acceptance have you experienced? The testimony of one who has been directly affected by God's love is powerful. You have a unique perspective and a story to tell. Don't believe for a moment that your voice or your experience doesn't matter.

There is an unrelenting wave of bad news. We don't have to look far to find it. But spreading good news reminds us that not all is lost. There is still goodness at work in the world. There are people fighting for change, for peace, and for justice. There is beauty around us. Let's dare to share the good things, not to cancel out the hard but to encourage our hope in the midst of it.

*Jesus, your mercy meets me in my little corner of the world, and I am changed. I will not stay silent about what you have done, for you are incredibly good. As the psalmist said, "Your tender love is blended into everything you do" (Psalm 145:9).*

## Joyful Reception

The news of this miracle of resurrection caused the crowds to swell as great numbers of people welcomed him into the city with joy.

JOHN 12:18

The news of Lazarus being resurrected after four days in the grave spread far and wide. It was a tremendous miracle, and it drew even greater crowds of people to see the One who had performed it. Can you relate to these people? Have you ever heard such incredible news about Jesus that it drew you to him?

The city was full of celebration as they welcomed Jesus with praise. It would not be long before the mood changed. Still, this is no reason to hold back joy when it fills us. We were created to celebrate the coming of the King. When we encounter his goodness, we should praise him for all that he has done and even more for who he is. With joy, we can celebrate his kindness toward us. Think of every reason you have to rejoice today and offer God praise sparked by the joy in your heart.

*Worthy One, thank you for the beauty of your love displayed in this world and in my life. I worship you!*

## Brave Surrender

"Let me make this clear: A single grain of wheat will never be more than a single grain of wheat unless it drops into the ground and dies. Because then it sprouts and produces a great harvest of wheat—all because one grain died."

JOHN 12:24

The cycles of nature teach us about the ways of God. A grain of wheat will never be more than just that unless it drops to the ground and dies. In its dying, it sprouts and produces a great harvest. If we are willing to surrender our own lives in love to a greater purpose, we will reap fruitfulness from our submission.

We cannot hold so tightly to our own comfort, trying to preserve our life as we know it, that we resist the changes that come with time. None of us can avoid the natural ends in jobs, relationships, or our very lives. Let's live with brave surrender, then, yielding to the will of God that guides us into his ways. Nothing goes wasted in the fields of his kingdom.

*Savior, I don't want to hold so dearly to my idea of a good life that I miss out on what you want to do. I yield to your loving leadership, trusting you to do more with the deaths and ends than I could ever imagine. You are always doing something new.*

## True Life

> "The person who loves his life and pampers himself will miss
> true life! But the one who detaches his life from this world and
> abandons himself to me, will find true life and enjoy it forever!"
>
> JOHN 12:25

True life is not found in pampering ourselves or reaching the pinnacle of success in the eyes of the world. It is found in abandoning ourselves to the love of Christ. In him, we find more satisfaction than we could ever conjure up on our own. No amount of money or privilege could buy us a level of soul-contentedness that we find in the incredible mercy of God. There is always a moving target in the world, but Christ meets us with peace, joy, hope, and love right where we already are.

Most of us can think of ways we keep ourselves sedated by the world. It does not mean that we have not given Christ any of our lives. However, there are, perhaps, more layers to shed and offer to Christ. If we want to live fully abandoned to Christ, we must be willing to prioritize the love of Christ—and, in turn, the compassion he compels us to move in—more than we do our comfort. He leads us into true life as we do.

*Christ, thank you for your powerful love that leads me into the abundance of your life. I don't want to be enslaved to anything in the world. I want to be motivated by you, Jesus, more than anything. I surrender to you.*

*Follow Him*

"If you want to be my disciple, follow me and you will go where I am going. And if you truly follow me as my disciple, the Father will shower his favor upon your life."

JOHN 12:26

Jesus walked with confidence into his destiny. He knew where he was going, and he offers to guide us through the trials of this world and into the eternal realm of his kingdom. Following him requires us to trust, take direction, and maintain a yielded heart. As we get to know him better, we discover how wonderfully kind, patient, and reliable he truly is.

Though we may regret taking on traditions that don't reflect the heart or truth of Christ, there is no regret in living for him. The person of Christ is liberating. He never abandons us. He is not judgmental or far away. He knows us perfectly, and he loves us all the same. He knows exactly what we need before we even ask. Instead of coming up with excuses to do our own thing today, let's lean into the presence of God and ask him to guide us through the twists and turns of our day.

*Jesus, you are better than I can comprehend. I believe that to be true. I will follow you because you are worthy and worth it.*

## *Even in Turmoil*

"Even though I am torn within, and my soul is in turmoil, I will not
ask the Father to rescue me from this hour of trial. For I have
come to fulfill my purpose—to offer myself to God."

JOHN 12:27

Jesus' soul was in great turmoil as he anticipated the betrayal, pain, and separation he would soon experience. Jesus knew what it was to deal with anxiety and still choose to surrender to God. He trusted his Father. The presence of courage does not require the absence of fear—exactly the opposite, in fact. Courage does not deny the presence of pain, anxiety, or fear. It recognizes it and still chooses to keep going and to do the hard thing.

You do not have to overcome the dread of something in order to surrender to God in the midst of it. In turmoil and pain lies your greatest sacrifice of praise. Psalm 42 offers us a beautiful example of a prayer of surrender. Read through it and offer it as your own prayer in the midst of emotional upheaval. Together with the psalmist, you can declare, "Just keep hoping and waiting on God, your Savior. For no matter what, I will still sing with praise, for you are my saving grace!" (v. 5).

*Lord, I surrender to you even in my greatest pain and turmoil.
I choose to trust.*

# A Voice Replies

"Father, bring glory to your name!" Then suddenly a booming voice was heard from the sky, "I have glorified my name! And I will glorify it through you again!"

JOHN 12:28

In his time of extreme need, the Father did not neglect Jesus. After Jesus had finished praying, a voice boomed from heaven in response. The voice reminded him of his ultimate purpose: redeeming humanity. This must have been an encouragement, helping him to maintain his focus on what lay beyond all the pain and suffering.

When you are in pain and turmoil, as Jesus was, cry out to God. God loves to meet you in the midst of your pain, not because he wants you to be in it but because he is the God of all comfort. "He is the Father of tender mercy…And just as we experience the abundance of Christ's own sufferings, even more of God's comfort will cascade upon us through our union with Christ" (2 Corinthians 1:3, 5). When troubles weigh us down, God offers us comfort and reminders of truth that shift our perspectives. He is oh so near no matter what we go through.

*Father, I want to know the comfort of your nearness today. Speak to me, Lord, and bring relief to my soul.*

# Thunderous Voice

The audible voice of God startled the crowd standing nearby.
Some thought it was only thunder, yet others said,
"An angel just spoke to him!"

JOHN 12:29

When God meets us in our pain, others may also witness the power of his comfort. The work he does in us and through our circumstances stands as testimony to his faithfulness. He has not left you alone to waste away in your anguish. He will not let fear conquer you. As David declared in Psalm 23:4, "[Lord,] even when your path takes me through the valley of deepest darkness, fear will never conquer me, for you already have!"

There is so much power in the persistent love of God over our lives. Even when we walk through the hardest situations in our lives, we are not alone. The thunderous voice of God rings out over our lives, and not only do we benefit from this, but those around us do too. As we bear witness to God's voice declaring his lordship over those around us, may we be encouraged to offer him praise and to offer others the encouragement of our witness.

*Great God, thank you for the power of your lordship over my life. I yield to you.*

## Help to Believe

Jesus told them, "The voice you heard was not for my benefit, but for yours—to help you believe."

JOHN 12:30

God knows exactly what we need, right when we need it. Jesus knew his mission, and though the Father's response was directed at him, the true benefit was to those who heard the thunderous voice. Jesus did not need help believing in his purpose, but perhaps the people around him did. God knows our hearts and minds and how quickly we forget his power. He graciously offers us confirmation of who he is just when we need it most.

Have you ever experienced this kind of help from God to believe in him? He still works in powerful, miraculous, and mysterious ways through his Spirit. He has not finished moving in mercy among us. He reveals himself to those who seek him. Those who had gathered around Jesus in those days became witnesses to the thunderous voice. They would carry this with them through the coming days of Jesus' trial and crucifixion. May we, with help from God, believe what he has said he will do.

*Jesus, thank you for your kindness and patience toward me. Help my belief and draw me closer to your heart. I believe in you.*

## Forever Changed

"From this moment on, everything in this world is about to change, for the ruler of this dark world will be overthrown. And I will do this when I am lifted up off the ground and when I draw the hearts of people to gather them to me."

JOHN 12:31–32

Have you ever been on the precipice of a life change and didn't know what to anticipate? Jesus knew what was coming for him, but he also knew the powerful feelings that accompany a huge transition. If you feel alone under the weight of what is coming, look to the One who already knows what lies ahead for you. You can trust him to be with you every step of the way.

Jesus walked through pain, suffering, and rejection, all to make a way for us to come to the Father through him. He overthrew the power of the enemy that seeks to steal, kill, and destroy. When we live under the lordship of Christ, we come alive in his victory over death. He is the Way, the Truth, and the Life. Let's follow him, for he is our Liberator and Savior.

*Jesus Christ, you changed everything when you went to the cross and rose from the grave. I trust you in every area of my life, for I come alive in your victory.*

## *Letting Go of Preconceptions*

People from the crowd spoke up and said, "Die? How could the Anointed One die? The Word of God says that the Anointed One will live with us forever, but you just said that the Son of Man must be lifted up from the earth. And who is this Son of Man anyway?"

JOHN 12:34

Sometimes the best thing we can do when following Christ is to let go of what we think we already know. The people in the crowd couldn't fathom the Anointed One dying. It wasn't at all what they expected. They knew the Scriptures that said the Anointed One would live with his people forever. They could not fathom another way.

If we are too focused on what we've believed to be true, we may miss the truth of what is. Christ is more powerful than death. Though he died, he rose again to life three days later. He vanquished the power of the grave and resurrected in freedom and victory. The person of Christ is more powerful than our ideologies about him. Let's be sure we are following him more closely than we follow our perceptions of him.

*Jesus, even when I don't understand your ways, I trust you as the Son of God. I believe in who you are more than I do my own understanding of you. Reveal to me the truth of your being in deeper ways today.*

## Embrace the Time

> Jesus replied, "You will have the light shining with you for only a little while longer. While you still have me, walk in the light, so that the darkness doesn't overtake you. For when you walk in the dark you have no idea where you're going."
>
> JOHN 12:35

Jesus, the Light of the World, was only on this earth for a mere thirty-three years. He ministered for about three of those years. It was not a long time, but it was significant, nonetheless. He showered the light of the Father wherever he went. He reflected the mercy of the Father through his interactions with others. He paid the ultimate price at the end so that we could all know the Father and live forever free in the kingdom of his love.

These lives we have are short. None of us knows how long we have on this earth. Let's make the most of it by spending time with those we love. There are beautiful lives of light all around us. We must embrace the little time we have with them. Today, instead of rushing through our tasks and to-do lists, let's make time for the lights in our own lives. This is not a waste but a valuable use of the time we have with each other.

*Jesus, thank you for those who reflect your love in my life. What a treasure they are to me!*

# Children of Light

"Believe and cling to the light while I am with you, so that you will become children of light." After saying this, Jesus then entered into the crowd and hid himself from them.

JOHN 12:36

It has been said that we become like those we behold. If we want to become like Christ, we must spend time with him. The more attention we give to the presence of God, the more we are transformed in its power. The more we look to Christ—to his nature, his values, and his priorities—the more deeply we understand who he is.

Like stars in the night sky, we reflect the light of the sun (Son). As he shines his light on us, our lives reflect his glory. We don't simply hear his Word or acknowledge his goodness, but we adopt them as our guidelines for living lives of sacrificial love. We have all been given something, no matter how little, to manage in this life. As we manage it with faithfulness and integrity, we are given greater responsibilities (see Luke 16:10). As we live in surrender to Christ's ways, we reflect the light of his glory.

*Lord, I believe and cling to all that you are not only with my words but also with my surrendered life. Have your way in me.*

# Set Free from Fear's Grip

There were many Jewish leaders who believed in Jesus, but because they feared the Pharisees they kept it secret, so they wouldn't be ostracized by the assembly of the Jews.

JOHN 12:42

The fear of others can cause you to hide your true beliefs from them. If you value acceptance and validation more than you do the conviction of your heart, you are allowing the grip of fear to keep you from the liberty of Christ's love. Conformity is not the way of Christ's kingdom. When you value what others think of you more than you do your own integrity, it is you who will suffer for it.

Do you dare lay down the need to please others or your attempts to live up to their expectations of you? If you continue in this way, you may find yourself a stranger in your own life, or you may be filled with resentment. Only you can choose how you will live. Only you can choose what you believe. Christ offers you freedom from fear in his love. Will you receive it and live it out?

*Christ Jesus, I don't want to live for others' comfort or satisfaction. Free me from people-pleasing and lead me into greater liberty from a place of integrity and conviction.*

# Looking for Validation

*They loved the glory that men could give them rather than the glory that came from God!*

JOHN 12:43

It is so important that we know the things we are living for, the motivations, the ambitions, and the goals. Whose goals are they? Are we trying to gain the approval of the world, or are we looking to live for the kingdom of Christ? Certainly a spectrum lies in between these two poles. Most of us are trying our best with what we have.

God's promises are better than the promises of this world. His affection is not contingent upon our performance. He loves us because he loves us. If we live for the glory that people can offer us, it will not last long before the objective has moved. The priorities of this world change almost as swiftly as the winds. The values of Christ's kingdom never change though. Let's live for what matters, for what lasts into eternity. When our identities are rooted in who God says we are, we build our lives on a firm foundation.

*Jesus, thank you for never changing your mind about me. Your love sets me free and gives me a path to follow that is steady, true, and lasting. I live for your glory, Lord.*

# Clear Picture of God

Jesus shouted out passionately, "To believe in me is to also believe in God who sent me. For when you look at me you are seeing the One who sent me."

JOHN 12:44–45

Jesus revealed what the Father is really like. Though the Jewish leaders thought they knew who God was, it was clear that many of them had no idea. They thought God was a rule follower. In Christ, we see that mercy is more important than the particulars of the law. Even so, Christ fulfilled every aspect of the law, meaning that the Jewish leaders missed out on the nature of God in the Scriptures, favoring instead tradition, control, and their places of power.

Religion may give us clues to what God is like, but following tradition more closely than the nature of God is dangerous. In the end, we may think we have done all there is to find God, but if we are unwilling to change our ways when presented with opportunities to show love that reaches beyond our comfort zones, we have our priorities out of whack. Look to Christ and find the beauty of God's loving-kindness. He is better than we could ever describe.

*Christ, I believe that you are the image of God in the flesh. It is you I follow more than any other thing, even those things done in your name. It is you.*

# No Longer Wandering

"I have come as a light to shine in this dark world so that all who trust in me will no longer wander in darkness."

JOHN 12:46

The light of Christ shines on us and clears up our confusion. The light of his love reveals what was once hidden in darkness. We are no longer wandering through life trying to feel our way around. There is no need to fear the shadows. As we put our total trust in Jesus Christ, he guides us into the goodness of his mercy-kindness.

Even when we cannot see our way through to the other side of our circumstances, that does not mean that we are wandering. Jesus, our Good Shepherd, guides us through nights of grief and suffering. He watches over us as we sleep. We are not outside of his gaze for even a moment. Take heart if you find yourself in a dark night of the soul. He is the light that shines on you still. Trust him even if you cannot see him. He has not nor will he ever leave you. He will guide you along peaceful paths that bring refreshment to your soul.

*Good Shepherd, thank you for the light that shines in the darkness. Even when I cannot sense you, I know you, and I know that you are near.*

## Wonderful Savior

"If you hear my words and refuse to follow them, I do not judge you. For I have not come to judge you but to save you."

JOHN 12:47

How many of us know those who are quick to judge? Perhaps we are the ones who quickly jump to conclusions. When others don't agree with us, our reactions reveal our own hearts. It is not hard to make judgments against others. It is far too easy, in fact. It takes intentionality, humility, and compassion to choose a different way.

When we lay down our judgments against others, we follow in the steps of Jesus. He is the only Wise Judge, and yet he said that he did not come to judge but to save. If Jesus does not condemn those who don't believe him, far be it from us to do it on his behalf. Remember Jesus' words in Matthew 7 when he said, "Refuse to be a critic full of bias toward others, and you will not be judged" (v. 1). Whatever measure we use will be used on us. What incentive to be gracious!

*Gracious Savior, help me to lay down my judgments and to give grace to others just as I hope to receive grace. Thank you.*

# Truth Will Be Our Judge

"If you reject me and refuse to follow my words, you already have a judge. The message of truth I have given you will rise up to judge you at the Day of Judgment."

JOHN 12:48

The truth will be our judge on the last day. The message of Christ's truth remains the standard by which all will be measured. If we all face the same judge with the same standard, far be it from any of us to claim ourselves as the arbiters of God's justice. We are called to be light, salt, and love. We are called as peacemakers. We are called to lay down our own biases and to follow the path of Christ's laid-down love.

As long as it is called "today," it is an opportunity to embrace Christ and follow his words. He transforms us in the power of his mercy and leads us as we lean on him. Never is it our place to judge on God's behalf. We are always called to extend kindness, to pursue peace, and to care for the vulnerable. This does not mean we will not call out injustice or require accountability from those who misuse their power. God knows our hearts, and he knows our trajectory. As we yield to him, he leads us with wisdom.

*Jesus, you are the Way, the Truth, and the Life. I choose to follow you.*

### *Full Measure*

Jesus knew that the night before Passover would be his last night on earth before leaving this world to return to the Father's side. All throughout his time with his disciples, Jesus had demonstrated a deep and tender love for them. And now he longed to show them the full measure of his love.

JOHN 13:1

K nowing that this was his last night on earth, Jesus prepared himself for what was to come. A large part of this preparation was spending time with his close friends and continuing to show them his deep and tender love for them. Jesus' love was not demanding. In fact, he showed the full measure of his love most accurately in his humble service.

The love of God is beyond beautiful. Its power is in what it offers. This is something that we can take on in our own lives and relationships. The power of our love lies in what it offers others. It is not self-seeking, proud, or quick to take offense. It is incredibly patient, consistently kind to all, a safe place of shelter, and larger than we can account for (see 1 Corinthians 13). Whenever our love runs dry, we return to the overflowing fountain of God's endless mercy to fill up. Out of the overflow, we have so much to offer.

*Jesus, thank you for your incredibly extravagant love. I receive it today.*

# Owning Your Influence

Jesus was fully aware that the Father had placed all things under his control, for he had come from God and was about to go back to be with him.

JOHN 13:3

Jesus knew who he was, and he knew the authority he had. He walked in the confidence of his identity as God's Son. We don't have to be divine to know who we are. Our identities are not in question. The King of kings and Lord of lords loves us. The Creator made us in his image, and we reflect his artistry in our lives.

Confidence does not equal pride. While pride protects our egos, or rather our ideas of who we are, confidence is rooted in the reality of who God says we are. It is not pride to know we are unconditionally loved and accepted as we are. It is not pride to be fully aware of our giftings or to use the authority we have in our respective jobs, spheres of influence, or communities. As we own who we are and the opportunities that are uniquely ours, we can confidently go about doing what is ours to do.

*Jesus, thank you for your hand of mercy on my life. Thank you for who I am in you and who you are in me. May my identity be firmly rooted in you.*

## Tender Affection

> He poured water into a basin and began to wash the disciples'
> dirty feet and dry them with his towel.
>
> JOHN 13:5

Jesus, the Son of God, the Worthy One, showed his love by taking on the lowliest position in the room. It was a servant's job to wash the dirty feet of diners. Jesus, humbling himself in a very real and practical way, picked up a towel and basin to serve his disciples in love.

Imagine the dirtiest job you have to do, and picture Jesus doing that for you. What if Jesus washed your toilet for you? What if he cleaned you up after you got sick? Think of how impactful that would be to you. Imagine how you might react at first. Love is as practical as it is emotional. It reveals itself through how we treat each other, what we do for one another, and the sacrifices we make. How can you show tender affection to someone in your life today?

*Humble Jesus, your love is big, powerful, and beautiful. It is also incredibly specific, practical, and identifiable. Thank you for the tender affection you show me. The more I recognize it, the more I can deliberately reach out in the same way to others.*

# Soon You Will See

Jesus replied, "You don't understand yet the meaning of what I'm doing, but soon it will be clear to you."

JOHN 13:7

Oftentimes when God moves, we do not sense or understand the meaning of it at first. His ways seem mysterious, and yet he reveals the power and purpose to us in time. Do we have the patience and trust to allow God to move without having to have a firm grasp of what he is doing?

Romans 8:28 says this: "We are convinced that every detail of our lives is continually woven together for good, for we are his lovers who have been called to fulfill his designed purpose." We can be convinced that God weaves the details of our lives together without our having to know exactly how. As we trust him, our hearts grow in confidence of his faithfulness. He is reliable and true. Though we "see but a faint reflection of riddles and mysteries…one day we will see face-to-face" (1 Corinthians 13:12).

*Lord Jesus, even when I don't understand your ways, I trust your heart. Do what you will, and I trust you to reveal the connections of your mercy as we journey together.*

# Let Him Wash over You

Peter looked at Jesus and said, "You'll never wash my dirty feet—never!" "But Peter, if you don't allow me to wash your feet," Jesus responded, "then you will not be able to share life with me."

JOHN 13:8

If we resist receiving God's mercy, then we won't be able to share life with him. We must allow him to wash over us with his tender affection. What a gracious offering this is! It cost him everything, and yet it is a gift for us to simply receive.

When was the last time you let the pure love of God wash over you? When you insist on bettering yourself on your own, you resist the incredible power of God's mercy to transform your life. His love is pure kindness, light, and life. It washes away the dirt of our sins, our fears, and our shame. We are made perfect in his love. What a wonderful mystery this is! First John 4:18 says, "Love never brings fear...but love's perfection drives the fear of punishment far from our hearts." Let's embrace this love as it washes over our hearts, minds, and souls today.

*Lord Jesus, wash me in your mercy and cleanse me in your righteousness. Thank you for the gracious gift of your mercy that makes me clean and sets me free.*

# Cleansed from the Dust

Jesus said to him, "You are already clean. You've been washed completely and you just need your feet to be cleansed—but that can't be said of all of you."

JOHN 13:10

As we walk through this world, our feet are bound to get dirty. Though most of us may remain clean, we need the rinse of the Spirit to wash the dirt off our feet. Have you ever felt this way? Perhaps you felt as if your whole being was contaminated by the world, yet Jesus spoke to you that it was only a simple washing of your feet that you needed.

As you spend time in the presence of God today, ask him to wash over you and remove the dust from your feet. Ask him to reveal to you if any other areas need your attention. He is good and reliable. His love does not miss a thing. Don't devalue yourself, thinking it's the holy thing to do. Jesus does not degrade you; rather, he washes over you to reveal the beauty that is already in you, dear one. Rise up in his love and allow him to lead you into what he has for you.

*Jesus, you have cleansed me from my unrighteousness, and I don't have to worry about what you think of me. Thank you. Give me even greater revelations of your love and the reality of who I am in you.*

*Life Lessons*

After washing their feet, he put his robe on and returned to his place at the table. "Do you understand what I just did?" Jesus said.

JOHN 13:12

When God moves, he also takes the time to teach us. He doesn't just leave us questioning his actions. Jesus, after he washed the disciples' feet, wanted to be sure they truly understood what the significance was. He does not discourage our questions; he wants our curiosity.

There are life lessons about God's mercy on the move in your life. When was the last time you asked Jesus the significance of what he was doing? Jesus always opened the door for his disciples' questions. He encouraged them to be inquisitive. He wanted them to understand the deeper meaning behind his ways. He does the same with you. Don't fear his response to your questions. He is much more open to your curiosity than are the institutions of this world. Lean in and let him teach you the meaning of the lessons he has for you.

*Teacher, thank you for being so gracious, patient, and intentional with your people. I'm so grateful for your loving intention and instruction. Teach me, Lord. I am listening.*

# Follow His Example

"If I'm your teacher and lord and have just washed your dirty feet, then you should follow the example that I've set for you and wash one another's dirty feet. Now do for each other what I have just done for you."

JOHN 13:14–15

We cannot overlook the importance of following the example of Christ. The Son of God humbled himself to wash his disciples' dirty feet. What dirty jobs can we do for one another? There are things that have to be done that nobody wants to do. Yet when we take the attitude of Jesus and venture to convey our love through practical acts of service, we reveal the love of God alive and working in us.

"Do for each other what I have just done for you." Serving others requires laying down our pride. The attitude that we are above certain tasks becomes obsolete. We cannot claim to love others the way God loves us and somehow think we are above doing the dirty work that life requires. Think of practical and specific ways you can follow the example of Christ's foot washing and serve others in love today.

*Jesus, your ways really are better than mine. I am not too good to serve my brother and sister. I recognize that there is no act of service too small or too large that it cannot reveal your love.*

*Timeless Truth*

"I speak to you timeless truth: a servant is not superior to his master, and an apostle is never greater than the one who sent him."

JOHN 13:16

When we value our status more than we do the love of Christ, it is a clear indicator that our values are out of alignment with Christ's kingdom. If we want to truly live for him, we will reflect his principles in our relationships, the way we work, and in what we are willing to do. We must not value how others perceive us more than we do God's opinion. We know that he sees our hearts. We cannot fool him even a little.

There is no glory in pretending we are something that we are not. We don't please God when we overlook the vulnerable and embrace the powerful. As long as our comfort, success, and perspectives are the ones that are most important to us, we will miss out on opportunities to grow in love. The good news is this: today is the day you can choose how you will live, what priorities you will keep, and whose opinion you will live for. Choose this day whom you will serve.

*Lord, may I never think that I'm above serving others the way that you did. You are my example. I honor you.*

# Enriched by Obedience

"Put into practice what I have done for you,
and you will experience a life of happiness
enriched with untold blessings!"

JOHN 13:17

Obedience can feel like a dirty word if others have used it against us. But Jesus' intentions toward us are always good and never for our harm. He does not seek to keep us in line but to set us free in his love. While the best that others can do in leadership falls short of pure love, God's leadership in our lives never does.

Our lives become enriched with blessings as we put into practice all that Christ has done for us. He never requires from us what he did not already willingly go through or offer. Obedience to him is not confining; it is liberating. Do we need strength to choose him? He offers us grace by his Spirit. Do we need compassion to compel us forward? He has it in droves. All that we need to practice what he did is found in his presence. We don't do any of it alone. Praise God!

*Lord, I choose to follow you because you are good, trustworthy, and you know what you are doing. Thank you for the incredible power of your love.*

## Open Reception

"Listen to this timeless truth: whoever receives the messenger I send receives me, and the one who receives me receives the Father who sent me."

JOHN 13:20

When we embrace the Spirit, we receive Christ himself. As we receive Christ, we embrace the Father too. This is the blessing of the Trinity. We have the fullness of God available to us right here and now through the Holy Spirit. Could there be anything more humbling or wonderful?

The messenger of Christ is his Spirit. This is not some finite offering to a few. The Spirit is sent to all who believe. He is alive, moving, and working in this world and in our lives. Why would we wait a moment longer to receive the fullness of God? Even if we have been walking with the Lord our entire lives, there is more to discover, more to know, and more to receive from him. There is no end to his goodness, and we get to dwell in his faithful love all the days of our lives. Are we taking advantage of this wonderful gift that is ours?

*Holy Spirit, I am open to you today. You are welcome to teach me, move me, and refine me. Reveal more of Christ and the Father to me as I experience your presence. I wait on you.*

# Deeply Moved

Jesus was moved deeply in his spirit. Looking at his disciples, he announced, "I tell you the truth—one of you is about to betray me."

JOHN 13:21

Jesus' relationship with his disciples affected him deeply. The thought of one of his closest friends betraying him moved him with profound emotion. Have you ever known the pain of a betrayal? Take comfort in the One who knows your heartbreak. He truly understands what you have been through.

Jesus knew the risk of relationship. In order to love, we have to choose to be vulnerable. It was no different with Jesus and his disciples. He knew the cost of betrayal better than anyone. It cost him his very life, and yet he did not withhold his love from his betrayer. We must not close ourselves off to love for fear of what could happen. If we protect ourselves from loss, we will also stay an arm's length from true connection. Love is worth the risk. Jesus lived this, and he can help us live it too.

*Jesus, I take comfort and courage in your experience with Judas. You chose to love him, even knowing what he would do. I don't want to miss out on true connection for fear of what-ifs. Help me, Lord.*

# Time Is Fleeting

"My dear friends, I only have a brief time left to be with you. And then you will search and long for me. But I tell you what I told the Jewish leaders: you'll not be able to come where I am."

JOHN 13:33

Time is so very short. What will we do with these brief, beautiful lives we have? Let's make the most of our days, choosing to live for what matters most to us. The values of our lives are our guideposts, but sometimes we can get so lost in the weeds of the details of life that we lose sight of the brevity of it all. Take some time to really check in with your whys today.

It can be helpful to make a list of the things you are spending your time doing these days. Don't forget to also record what you want others to know of your life after you're gone. Now, go through each of these and consider what you can do less of and what you can incorporate more of to get more in line with your values. There is no better time than now to take stock of your life. The Spirit of wisdom is available to help you, so if you are at a loss, ask for insight and direction.

*Spirit, I want to live for what matters. Help me to make changes that will allow for that to happen.*

# September

## The Great Commandment

> "I give you now a new commandment:
> Love each other just as much as I have loved you."
>
> JOHN 13:34

When we ask the question, how far should we go in caring for one another, Jesus already gave us the clear answer: "Love each other just as much as I have loved you." He left no excuses for our lack of love. How much grace should we offer each other? The same amount that Christ offers us. How many times should we forgive those who keep offending us? As many times as they do it.

None of us will do this perfectly, and perfection is, quite frankly, not the point. Peter instructed that we "constantly echo God's intense love for one another, for love will be a canopy over a multitude of sins" (1 Peter 4:8). Love is the highest law in the realm of Christ's kingdom, and it should be ours, as well. If we are moving in love toward one another, we will find that petty arguments become less important. Love is the standard, and it always will be. We will never grow out of it.

*Lord over all, when I make excuses for my lack of love, bring me back to this. Ground me in your limitless mercy. It's all that matters.*

## Love Demonstrates Identity

"When you demonstrate the same love I have for you by loving one another, everyone will know that you're my true followers."

JOHN 13:35

How will people know that we are followers of Christ? Is it by our political leanings or theological bent? No. Is it through the arguments we win or the lack of problems we have in our lives? Again, no. Our bank accounts are also poor reflections of our allegiance to heaven. The way we reveal that we are true followers of Christ is simple and often overlooked: how we love one another.

If we love our perspectives more than we love our neighbors, we are getting it wrong. If we believe that our display of God's disapproval toward another is the way of Christ's kingdom, we've got some learning to do. The love of Christ living in and through us is the key identifier of the followers of Christ. That is what it all comes down to, no ifs, ands, or buts about it. What excuses can you lay down today in favor of actively loving those around you?

*Merciful God, I admit that this is easier said than done. Help me to love others well and to lay down the things that hinder love in my life.*

# He Knows Us Better

Jesus answered, "Would you really lay down your life for me, Peter? Here's the absolute truth: Before the rooster crows in the morning, you will say three times that you don't even know me!"

JOHN 13:38

Peter was sure of his own steadfast and zealous love for Christ. He refused to believe that he could ever deny knowing his teacher and friend. When Jesus confronted his friend in truth, he did not berate him. He simply told him what would happen. Peter was rather self-righteous in his opinion of himself. Soon, he would be humbled under the weight of his own denial.

Jesus knows us better than we know ourselves. He sees the potential for both good and bad within us. He does not judge our failures, but he does lovingly correct and guide us when we humble ourselves before him. He is steadfast in love, no matter how far we fall. May we yield to his loving leadership, especially when we fail to reach our own expectations. He is so much better and more gracious than we could dream of being.

*Gracious Lord, thank you for your mercy that covers my greatest failures. Help me to be humble rather than self-righteous. I want to reflect that love in my own relationships.*

## *Trust Him*

"Don't worry or surrender to your fear.
For you've believed in God,
now trust and believe in me also."

JOHN 14:1

The disciples were probably feeling fear as Jesus gave his parting words to his friends. They were hearing about betrayal and denial. They had not faced this before, and to hear their Master talk about such things must have made them feel the weight of what was to come. Jesus encouraged them, however, to not surrender to their fear.

What have you been worried about lately? Perhaps there is heavy news that you just cannot escape. Maybe great unknowns with big old question marks hang over your future. Take the words of Jesus to heart today: "Don't worry or surrender to your fear." He is with you in every twist and turn you face. He already knows your future, and you can trust him to help you through everything you're up against. He is God, and he is faithful.

*Jesus, I trust you with my present, and I trust you with my future. Even through the scary things that feel as if they're looming ahead, you are good, and I trust you to guide me through it all.*

# A Place to Rest

"My Father's house has many dwelling places.
If it were otherwise, I would tell you plainly,
because I go to prepare a place for you."

JOHN 14:2

In the kingdom of heaven, Christ prepares a place for us. There is room for all who come to him. Far be it from us to think that he would say one thing and do another. He is always faithful. The kingdom of Christ is not exclusive. It is open to all who come to him. He will never turn away a seeking heart.

Even when we struggle to find rest in this life, there is a place of eternal rest in the presence of the Father. When we graduate from this life, we enter into the actual fullness of the kingdom of our God. He graciously gives glimpses of this peace in our fellowship with the Spirit, who lives inside us. Even so, we cannot escape the trials of this life. One day, we will be free from pain, worry, sickness, and death. This is the place of rest that Christ prepares for us even now.

*Jesus, thank you for the open invitation to your kingdom. I come to you with a heart that needs reprieve. Meet me with the peace of your presence even as my hope looks forward to the fullness that is yet to come.*

*Where He Is*

"When everything is ready, I will come back and take you to myself so that you will be where I am."

JOHN 14:3

When everything is ready, Jesus will return. He promises to take us to be with him where he dwells. Though we see in part now, we will one day see everything fully. As 1 Corinthians 13 puts it, "Our present knowledge and our prophecies are but partial, but when love's perfection arrives, the partial will fade away…One day I will understand everything, just as everything about me has been fully understood" (vv. 9–10, 12).

If you find yourself longing for that day, count yourself in good company. In the meantime, we have the Spirit of God dwelling with us, and that is no consolation prize. Though we can't see the Spirit, we know the fruit of his presence. Though we cannot touch him, he somehow touches the depths of our spirits. Until Christ returns to make all wrong things right and usher us into the place where he is, we have the Spirit right where we are. What a glorious gift!

*Lord, thank you for the promise of your return and for the gift of your Spirit's presence. I belong to you, and I rely on you.*

# You Know the Way

"You already know the way to the place
where I'm going."

JOHN 14:4

Jesus made no small thing of revealing the power of his purpose and presence among his disciples. He came to set the captive free, to remove the barriers that stood between us and God, and to lead us into the fullness of fellowship with him. We have no further to look than Christ's words to find the answer to where Christ went.

Not only did Christ make it clear where he was going, but he had also already taught his followers how to get there. Whoever yields their life in faith to the Son of God, believing what he came to accomplish and adopting his love as their own, these are the ones who will follow in his footsteps. We see this in Scripture, and we can watch it play out in our lives, as well. Christ, our holy and beloved Savior, is the Way that makes us right with God and at peace in our very souls.

*Lord, you are the Way, you are the Truth, and you are the Life. It's you! There is no other way to the Father, the fullness of all life. I surrender to you, my beloved Lord.*

## Blessed Union

Jesus explained, "I am the Way, I am the Truth, and I am the Life. No one comes next to the Father except through union with me. To know me is to know my Father too."

JOHN 14:6

Jesus is the true reality of God with us, God among us, God poured out for us. When we come to God the Father through Christ, we experience the union of Father, Son, and Spirit. Jesus does more than simply take us to heaven; he brings us alongside the Father. The destination is not just heaven. It is the Father himself.

Union with God is not something to strive for. It is offered to us through Christ. Fellowship with our Creator is a gift that he freely gives. We enter through the Way; Christ is the doorway to the Father's presence. We follow the Truth; he is the living embodiment of God's ways. We come alive in the Life; he is the source of all that we need.

*Jesus, thank you for being the Way to the Father. I come through you to the presence of the Almighty, and I find myself coming alive in all that you are.*

## Glorious Revelations

*"From now on you will realize that you have seen him and experienced him."*

JOHN 14:7

Through fellowship with Christ, we have already seen and experienced the Father. What a glorious revelation! We have not been given limited access either. Christ is the gateway to the fullness of God's presence.

When the Spirit reveals the depths of the truth of God's goodness and greatness, we cannot help but be caught up in wonder. When was the last time you felt this awe come over you? There is more where that came from. There is always more to discover in the wonders of his glorious reality. Look to Jesus and find the answer to your heart's desire as he washes over you with understanding you could not conjure up on your own. He really is as wonderful as you hope, in fact, even more so!

*Glorious Father, thank you for glorifying your Son and revealing your character through him. I cannot help but be in awe of your limitless kindness and powerful goodness. Astound me in new ways with the truth of who you are as I look to you today.*

## Don't Miss It

"Don't you believe that the Father is living in me and that I am living in the Father? Even my words are not my own but come from my Father, for he lives in me and performs his miracles of power through me."

JOHN 14:10

The very proof of Jesus' identity was in the miracles of power that he performed. No one could find anything wrong with his ministry. Even the religious leaders who were threatened by his influence could not find any ways in which Jesus contradicted the truth of God's Word. He had an answer for every one of their objections.

We can miss what we're looking for when we remain too focused on the future. We need to pay attention to the here and now. God is with us—Father, Son, and Spirit—right now. He is moving in mercy in our yielded lives. Let's look to him and ask the Spirit to show us how his life is transforming our own. Remember Jesus' words in John 5:17 when he said, "Every day my Father is at work, and I will be, too!"

*Father, open my eyes to see how you are working in my life. I look to you.*

## *Reason to Believe*

"Believe that I live as one with my Father and that my Father lives as one with me—or at least, believe because of the mighty miracles I have done."

JOHN 14:11

The more we get to know who Christ is through his ministry, his relationships, and through his character, the clearer it becomes that Jesus is unlike other men. He did not bow to religious institutions, nor did he promote himself within the local government. Everything he did centered around one thing: his relationship with the Father.

There are practical reasons to believe that Jesus is the Son of God, just as there are mystical ones. Even if it were difficult to believe that Jesus was the Son of God simply through his teachings, the mighty miracles he performed back up his testimony. You don't have to experience the power of God in miraculous ways to believe in him, but it certainly can help you get over the hurdle of doubt. In what practical ways has God revealed his wonderful kindness in your life?

*Merciful Father, I'm grateful for the power of your love in my life revealed through very real answers to prayer. I cannot begin to thank you enough.*

## Promises of Faith

> "I tell you this timeless truth: The person who follows me in faith, believing in me, will do the same mighty miracles that I do—even greater miracles than these because I go to be with my Father!"
>
> JOHN 14:12

Jesus promised that when we follow him in faith, we would do the same miracles that he did. How many of us experience this? How many of us truly believe this? We are the ministry of Jesus left on the earth. His Spirit empowers us in love, causing us to reach out to others. If we fail to realize our mission—our commission—is from Jesus, we cannot fulfill it.

The disciples went on to move in the power of the Spirit, but Jesus' words were not for them alone. The promises of following Christ in faith are for everyone who takes the Lord at his word. When we lay down our lives before him and take up his cause, his love becomes the compelling force behind everything we do. We learn to engage with people in the same way and offer the miracle of God's power to change lives. What a calling!

*Miracle Worker, I want to walk in your footsteps. Spirit, move in and through my surrendered life.*

# Ask Anything

"I will do whatever you ask me to do when you ask me in my name. And that is how the Son will show what the Father is really like and bring glory to him. Ask me anything in my name, and I will do it for you!"

JOHN 14:13–14

Have you ever talked yourself out of asking for something that you actually wanted? Denying desire is not necessary with God. He wants all of us, just as we are. We can give him all that we are and still submit to him.

Jesus was clear when he said, "Ask me anything in my name, and I will do it for you." We must not be afraid to tell him what is on our hearts. Let's not hold back for fear of being misunderstood. He knows our hearts, honors our desires, and answers our prayers. And even when our prayers aren't answered exactly as we expect, we can trust him. He knows best, and he does not require that we be perfect in how we approach him. Give him your full, undiluted heart today, and don't hold back a thing.

*Jesus, thank you for welcoming me just as I am. I won't hold myself back from you in the least today. No fear, no shame, and no lack of belief will keep me from pouring out my whole heart to you. I am asking as a child asks his trustworthy and beloved parent.*

## Empowered by Love

"Loving me empowers you to obey my commands."
JOHN 14:15

L ove is the source of all that we need. Love is the source of everything. John said, "The one who doesn't love has yet to know God, for *God is love*" (1 John 4:8, emphasis added). What wonderful news it is that the love that empowers us to obey is the love that God first poured out on us. He offers us himself, and we get to show our gratitude by pouring out that same love in obedience to his Word.

Love for Christ is revealed in our obedience to all that he says. Simply put, if we love Christ, then our lives will show it. Love without trust doesn't get us very far. Neither does love without action. First John 5:3 says it this way, "True love for God means obeying his commands, and his commands don't weigh us down as heavy burdens." It is a joy to obey him because he is faithful, he is for us, and he is with us through it all.

*Jesus, I love you because you first loved me. It really is that simple. It is my joy to walk in your ways and obey your Word.*

# *Home of the Spirit*

"I will ask the Father and he will give you another Savior, the Holy Spirit of Truth, who will be to you a friend just like me—and he will never leave you. The world won't receive him because they can't see him or know him. But you know him intimately because he remains with you and will live inside you."

JOHN 14:16–17

The Holy Spirit is not just our Counselor. He is our Comforter, Advocate, Encourager, Intercessor, and Helper. He is the Holy Spirit of Truth, our Defender against our enemies and sometimes against even ourselves. The Spirit finishes the work of Christ in our lives and saves us from the effects of sin. He is God within us, never leaving us for a moment.

What a beautiful and mystical promise it is that God makes his home inside us. Spirit to spirit, we fellowship with the King of kings. Though the world can't see or know him, we know him intimately within the depths of our beings. Every believer has become the home of the Holy Spirit. Not one of God's children is left out. Hallelujah!

*Spirit, you are welcome here, in me. Make yourself at home in my inner being and direct me. Thank you for your ministry, your power, and your comfort. I love you.*

## Never Abandoned

"I promise that I will never leave you helpless or abandon you as orphans—I will come back to you!"

JOHN 14:18

The answer to the promise of Christ to his disciples was threefold. He would come to them after his resurrection numerous times before he ascended to the Father. He would send the person of the Holy Spirit at Pentecost to live forever within them. Lastly, he will come in the day we still anticipate: the second coming.

Just as Jesus did not leave his disciples as orphans, he will not abandon any of us either. His ever-present Spirit stays with us through the good and the bad. He does not leave us alone in our trials or in our triumphs. He is with us. The Spirit's companionship is a glimpse of what it will be like when we are in the fullness of Christ's kingdom, wrapped in his love and living freely before the light of his face. What a day we await!

*Lord, thank you for promising to come back. Your Spirit's presence is my delight and my help, and I cannot thank you enough.*

## Come Alive

"Soon I will leave this world and they will see me no longer,
but you will see me, because I will live again,
and you will come alive too."

JOHN 14:19

In Christ's life, we come alive. His presence revives every part of our being. No matter how little or long it's been since we've spent time being refreshed in the company of Christ, this present moment is yet another opportunity to come alive in him. We can pray as the psalmist did: "May streams of your refreshing flow over us until our dry hearts are drenched again" (Psalm 126:4) and again and again! There is no end to the living waters of his love.

First John 4:17 says this: "By living in God, love has been brought to its full expression in us so that we may fearlessly face the day of judgment, because all that Jesus now is, so are we in this world." All that Jesus is—the fullness of his life—is what we are in this world. We are filled with the life of Christ, living out the wonders of his love from the never-ending source of his presence.

*Jesus, thank you for awakening me in your presence. Fill me afresh, rejuvenate my heart, and overflow my life, Lord.*

# Manifest Love

"Those who truly love me are those who obey my commands. Whoever passionately loves me will be passionately loved by my Father. And I will passionately love him in return and will reveal myself to him."

JOHN 14:21

The passionate love of Christ reaches out to your need today. His love is not lacking. It is not a weak trickle. It is a raging river careening toward you. This is the kind of love with which God fuels your own heart.

Have you been lacking passion in your heart toward God? Look at your life. Have you been following Christ's ways and living out his values? Do you treat people with kindness and grace? You don't always have to feel a hot, burning desire in order to be passionate. Your committed lifestyle is a passionate display of love toward God. Don't undervalue what God values most: a submitted life that reflects his love.

*God, may my life be a clear and steady reflection of your love and your values. You are the one I value more than any other. Be glorified in my life!*

# *Dwelling Places of the Almighty*

Jesus replied, "Loving me empowers you to obey my word. And my Father will love you so deeply that we will come to you and make you our dwelling place."

JOHN 14:23

The deep love of the Father for his children was the reason Christ came in the first place. Even back to the beginning of creation, the Father breathed the first people into existence with the breath of his affection. Not one day has passed before or since that God was not full of a deep, abiding, passionate love for us.

The Spirit is at home in those who put their faith in Christ. God has made his people his dwelling place. He is not bound by time, space, or tradition. He cannot be put in a box of our own making. He appeared to the Israelites as a cloud by day and a fire by night, but he was always much more than that. Our Creator invites us to expand our understanding and our being in the presence of his Spirit within us. Love always brings release and relief, while fear constricts and binds. As his dwelling places, we are filled with his love. May we follow his lead.

*Father, thank you for making your dwelling place in my heart. I am undone that I am a host to your presence.*

## Spirit of Holiness

"When the Father sends the Spirit of Holiness, the One like me who sets you free, he will teach you all things in my name. And he will inspire you to remember every word that I've told you."

JOHN 14:26

The Spirit of God teaches us and brings to remembrance all that we have already learned of the truth. He is a holy help. This is good news for those of us who feel the pressure to remember everything as it was. We can give up the fight for perfection and rely on the help of the Spirit to teach us what we do not yet know and to remind us of what we already do.

The Spirit of Holiness is like Jesus, teaching us and setting us free. He said it himself! If we question what is leading us at any given moment, we have only to look at the life of Christ to see whether it aligns or not. We also know the fruit of God's nature. He does not divide; he unites. He does not shame; he forgives. He does not shut others down; he opens up a conversation. May we walk in the confidence that the Helper will be there to guide us when we don't know which way to turn or what to do.

*Spirit, thank you for taking off my plate the responsibility of remembering everything. I listen to you.*

# Perfect Peace

"I leave the gift of peace with you—my peace. Not the kind of fragile peace given by the world, but my perfect peace. Don't yield to fear or be troubled in your hearts—instead, be courageous!"

JOHN 14:27

Most of us know the sting of a fragile peace that the world is adept at giving. Ceasefires are no guarantee of peace. The peace that Christ offers is much better. It is strong, unyielding even. It is perfect peace. Isaiah 26:3 says, "Perfect, absolute peace surrounds those who imaginations are consumed with you; they confidently trust in you."

Confident trust is a reflection of a strong bond to a reliable person. God is faithful, and he will never go back on his word. Jesus, the Prince of Peace, offered us this bit of advice: "Don't yield to fear or be troubled in your hearts…be courageous." The peace of God is the foundation of our courage. We have no need to yield to fear because our confident trust is in the one who conquered the grave and broke the power of sin over us.

*Prince of Peace, I receive your peace anew. Your peace is perfect, deep, and it isn't dependent on my circumstances. I won't yield to fear, for you are my Savior and my God.*

## Don't Forget

"Remember what I've told you, that I must go away, but I promise to come back to you. So if you truly love me, you will be glad for me, since I'm returning to my Father, who is greater than I. So when all of these things happen, you will still trust and cling to me."

JOHN 14:28–29

Jesus knows how quickly we forget words spoken to us. Who of us cannot relate to the disciples' need for reassurance and reminders? Even though the disciples did not realize the extent of what Jesus was saying, they would look back and see how wise and forthright he was in his foretelling of his death and subsequent resurrection.

How patient Christ is to offer to remind us of his promises and plans. He also brings to mind wisdom that we might have lost sight of. The Spirit of Christ does all this as we listen for his voice. As he reminds us of his Word, we have more of him to cling to and trust. He truly is patient with us. Let's heed the reminders he gives us today, knowing it is for the strengthening of our faith.

*Jesus Christ, you know how quickly I forget how you move. Bring to mind all that I need to remember today to stand strong in you.*

# The Pure One

"I won't speak with you much longer, for the ruler of this dark world is coming. But he has no power over me, for he has nothing to use against me."

JOHN 14:30

Jesus was the pure Lamb of God. Though the enemy caused many to turn against him and put him to death, Jesus was still more powerful than him. Jesus willingly laid down his life to fulfill every prophecy spoken about him and to break the curse of sin and death once and for all. Jesus did not fight those who fought him, but in the end, he was the victorious one.

When others bring all sorts of false accusations against us, we can stand strong in the truth of our innocence. Just as Jesus overcame the grave, so will we overcome the struggles we face and stand in his victory. Even if we suffer for a little while, God will never forsake us. In the end, we will stand with him in glory, and he will clear our names. Don't forget that the most important identity we have is that of children of God. Follow the example of Jesus and don't attack those who fight you. Their motives will be uncovered as time reveals their true colors.

*Holy One, I lay down my need for others to see me as right, and I simply follow you. I trust that the loudest voice is not always the one that wins in the end.*

## True Vine

"I am a true sprouting vine, and the farmer who tends the vine is my Father. He cares for the branches connected to me by lifting and propping up the fruitless branches and pruning every fruitful branch to yield a greater harvest."

JOHN 15:1–2

The word picture of Jesus being the true vine, the Father being the farmer who tends the vine, and his followers as branches that are connected to the vine illustrates how we can do nothing on our own. It also indicates that there are different kinds of vines in the world. If Jesus is the true vine, then there must also be imposters out there who, when we connect to them, cause us to bear different kinds of fruit.

There is no better source than Christ to be connected to. The Father lovingly lifts us up off the ground when we fail. This enhances our growth and our fruit-bearing ability. There is so much tenderness in his care. Jesus is the source that fills our lives with the nourishment we need to grow strong and bear fruit that reveals our identity. What a gloriously good God, to feed us with himself!

*Life Source, I don't want to fight for my way in the world. I receive the nourishment you offer. May the growth in my life reflect your work in me.*

## Remain Connected

"You must remain in life-union with me, for I remain in life-union with you. For as a branch severed from the vine will not bear fruit, so your life will be fruitless unless you live your life intimately joined to mine."

JOHN 15:4

Jesus does not simply require that we believe in him casually. He wants us to live intimately joined with him, grafted into his nature. We need to do nothing on our own. In fact, we cannot bear any lasting fruit apart from him. The answer to reflecting Christ is not to work harder; it is to fellowship with him. When we give up our striving, we can simply receive what he offers us and go from there.

Let your focus come back to the relationship between you and God today. Instead of getting caught up in what you should do for him, spend time in his presence *with* him. Consider the difference between running on a battery and plugging straight into a power source. One will fade with time, while the other will continue to feed off the energy of the source. There's no need to run low today. Plug into the source of true life.

*Jesus, I let go of my need to prove myself, and instead, I rest in you. I let you do what only you can do in and through me. I am yours.*

## Source of Fruitfulness

"I am the sprouting vine and you're my branches. As you live in union with me as your source, fruitfulness will stream from within you—but when you live separated from me you are powerless."

JOHN 15:5

The life of Christ branches out through his people. His life in us is what bears fruit. If we want our lives to reflect the power of his love, we must yield to him, remaining dependent on him as our source of all things. He is the source of wisdom, of strength, and of love. He is all that we need and so much more!

What fruit is evident in your life? Can you see the mark of Christ's mercy in and through you? Lean into his love today. Let union with Christ be the goal you reach for; it is so attainable. Whenever you think of it today, turn your attention to Christ within you. Ask him to move through you, to guide you with his wisdom, and to empower you to obey his words. You are a container of his glory, a conduit of his love. Live like it!

*Christ, be glorified in and through my surrendered heart and life. Your ways are my guideposts, and your love is the source of my strength. Thank you.*

## Abundant Fruit

"When your lives bear abundant fruit,
you demonstrate that you are my mature disciples
who glorify my Father!"

JOHN 15:8

How do we know that we glorify the Father? By the fruit our lives bear. Galatians 5 tells us what the fruit of the Spirit is like: "divine love in all its varied expressions" (vv. 22–23). Joy, peace, patience, kindness, goodness, prevailing faith, gentleness, and strength of spirit are the fruit that reveal the Spirit's work in our lives.

What kind of fruit is evident in your life? Perhaps you recognize some of the Spirit fruit Paul mentioned. Maybe you see other fruit that isn't so life-giving. It is not too late to change the way you live. Humble yourself before the Lord, allow the Spirit to move within you and refine you, and walk in the wisdom of Christ. As you do, your life will reveal the good fruit of God's mercy.

*Spirit, I don't want to get so caught up in my ideas of what is important and neglect the power of your practical mercy that is meant to be lived out. I submit to you and choose to walk in the ways of Christ, my Savior.*

## Nourished by Love

"I love each of you with the same love that the Father loves me. You must continually let my love nourish your hearts."

JOHN 15:9

We cannot overstate the love of God for us. In fact, all too often, we understate it. It can be easy to let love become a rote cliché, and yet it is the source of all that we need to nourish, refresh, and strengthen us. It is the creative spark we look for. It is the rest we long for. It is the wonder of creation. It is the marvel of human connection. It is so much more than all we could imagine it to be.

If you do nothing else today, let the love of Christ nourish your heart. If there is anything that draws your attention back over and over again throughout your day, may it be the lavishly present affection your God has for you. Love will lift you up. It will make you soar. It will rush over you like a river, and it will send you to where you are meant to go. Love will give you the strength and courage to face whatever comes. It is the nourishment that will sustain you through droughts. Open up and receive the satisfying and transformative love of God. There is a fresh portion for you right here and now.

*Loving God, it is too much for me to understand the influence of your love, and yet I've seen its miraculous power in my life. I feast on your love yet again. Thank you.*

## In the Same Way

"If you keep my commands, you will live in my love, just as I have kept my Father's commands, for I continually live nourished and empowered by his love."

JOHN 15:10

Jesus knew that love is more than a feeling. It is more than a tender pull toward the objects of our affection. It is dedication, loyalty, and follow-through. It is honor, respect, and reliability. It is all these things and more. If Jesus, the Son of God, kept his Father's commands as an act of love, how much more should we obey him? If we love and trust him, it is our pleasure to do what he asks of us. It is our honor to partner with him on the earth and in our lives.

Empowered by love, we live out the ways of Christ, knowing that everything he tells us to do is out of a place of love. Not only this, but the foundation of his love is truth. He is not living in an alternate reality. His truth is the foundation of the universe. If we know that God sees everything clearly as it is, and he offers his wisdom to guide us through this life, there is no better thing than to trust him and follow his guidance.

*Jesus, I keep your commands because I know that you are trustworthy and true.*

# Overflowing Joy

"My purpose for telling you these things is so that the joy that I experience will fill your hearts with overflowing gladness!"

JOHN 15:11

Following God is not meant to suck the joy out of our lives. On the contrary—God is full of delight! He is a joyful God who laughs with the best of them. Joy is not a consolation prize for pain. The joy of God is not subpar to the joy you experience in this world. It is infinitely better. It is true and unadulterated. It flows from the heart of God.

If you have trouble connecting to this joy, think about the way the sun rises in the morning and sets in the evening. God takes delight in his creation. There is so much beauty. Every sunrise is its own magic. The sun sets slightly differently each evening, and yet it is glorious. The way trees move with the wind and waves crash against the shore, it's a work of art. Our Creator is not a tortured artist but a joyful one. May you know the overwhelming gladness of God rising up within you as you take in his practical love today.

*Creator, I am in awe of your creation. Your creativity and pleasure are all over it. Fill me with your joy as I live for you. You are my deep delight.*

## Measure of Love

"This is my command: Love each other deeply,
as much as I have loved you."

JOHN 15:12

The greatest command in the entire Bible is found in this verse. We are to love each other the same way that Christ loves us. You might wonder when it's okay to set this command aside. Love does not rejoice in wrongdoing but in the truth (see 1 Corinthians 13:6). It does, however, display patience, forgiveness, and honor. We don't have to like everyone to offer them the dignity of Christ's love.

Remember Jesus' words in John 13:35? He said, "When you demonstrate the same love I have for you by loving one another, everyone will know that you're my true followers." The way that the world will know that we are followers of Christ is by the love we display for one another. When we overlook offenses and extend mercy, we reflect Christ in our love. When we take care of each other and bear one another's burdens, we show that the love of Christ is active in our lives. Let's look for ways to love others deeply, not for ways out of it.

*Jesus, your love is the standard. I choose to follow you on your path of love, leaving the excuses of humanity behind. Love is worth the cost.*

# Greatest Love of All

"The greatest love of all is a love that sacrifices all.
And this great love is demonstrated
when a person sacrifices his life for his friends."

JOHN 15:13

The greatest love is displayed through sacrifice. Have you ever had someone give up something of great value for you? What impact did that have on your life? God demonstrated most clearly the immense beauty of his love through the sacrifice Jesus made on the cross. God's love did not stop at taking on human form or performing miracles. It allowed people's hearts to turn to their Creator. It underwent the pain of death in order to free us from death's curse. What lengths does God's love reach even now!

Jesus did not sacrifice his life only for his friends. He sacrificed his life for everyone, for those who blessed and cursed him alike. He took the weight of our sin, our shame, and our fear, and he allowed death to take his body. Thankfully, that was not the end of the story. He rose again in victory, liberating us from the grip of sin and death, and setting us free in his resurrection power.

*Jesus, your love has no match, and yet I want to live by its standard in every area of my life. Fill me with your love so that it may overflow and empower my choices today.*

# Christ's Ways

"You show that you are my intimate friends
when you obey all that I command you."

JOHN 15:14

Christ did not give us weighty expectations that we could never fulfill. His commands don't deplete our love, for they lead us back to his love. Everything he does is wise, and everything he asks us to do is with purpose. Though we may not understand the meaning of it all, may we trust the One who asks us to do it.

The ways of Christ lead to peace, joy, and freedom. They are not burdensome. He offers to help us lift the load we already carry through this life, and he offers us the lightness of his ways. Though love costs us something, it is not without its reward. Sacrifice and surrender don't sound joyful, and yet when we give them to God, there is no joy greater. He is worthy of our obedience, but it need not be blind obedience. He welcomes us into fellowship with him. He welcomes our questions. All of us are welcome in him. What a delight it is, then, to offer him ourselves in return.

*Jesus Christ, there is nothing greater than to know you. Draw me deeper into friendship with you as I follow your will and ways.*

## Intimate Friendship

"I have never called you 'servants,' because a master doesn't confide in his servants, and servants don't always understand what the master is doing. But I call you my most intimate and cherished friends, for I reveal to you everything that I've heard from my Father."

JOHN 15:15

Jesus doesn't withhold the Father's heart from any of his friends. What a beautiful relationship we have with him! We are not his servants; we are his friends. He shares what he has with us, and reciprocating, we share what we have with him.

Up until this point, only the great prophets were considered friends with God. Abraham and Moses were known this way. Jesus made friendship with the Almighty accessible to each and every one of us. Which is the greater mystery: the fact that we can be friends with God or that he chooses to be friends with us? The next time you question your worth, remember that God both invites you into intimate fellowship with him and calls you friend.

*Jesus, thank you for your friendship. It is an honor to know you and be known by you. I only want to grow closer to you.*

# Chosen

"You didn't choose me, but I've chosen and commissioned you to go into the world to bear fruit. And your fruit will last, because whatever you ask of my Father, for my sake, he will give it to you!"

JOHN 15:16

Before you could even think of choosing to follow Christ, he chose you as his own. You were in his heart long before you knew his name. He has watched you blossom and grow. Your Creator did not stop at your conception. He knows your name, and he pursued you with passion long before you felt your heart come alive in his presence.

You are chosen, beloved. You are the apple of your Father's eye. He is not disappointed in you. Even in the ways that you have fallen short, he does not hold even one of those things against you. He loves you. He longs to meet you, revive you, and transform you in his love. Chosen one, turn to the One who calls your name today. It is not too late to come to him surrendering all that you thought you wanted but that only disappointed you in the end. You are his beloved child. Come and be restored in his living mercy.

*Father, I am undone at the power of your love for me. I choose you, Lord, knowing good and well that you chose me first.*

# Lay Down Allegiance

"If you were to give your allegiance to the world, they would love and welcome you as one of their own. But because you won't align yourself with the values of this world, they will hate you. I have chosen you and taken you out of the world to be mine."

JOHN 15:19

If you define yourself more by your political leanings than your relationship with God, Christ has something to say about it. If you find that you favor those who have the same preferences as you do, wake up and hear what Jesus is saying. God doesn't ask us to give allegiance to any systems in this world. In fact, he warns us against it. When we give our allegiance to the world and its systems, we will find places of belonging but only as long as we don't step out of line.

The kingdom of God does not value what this world values: power, prestige, and personal autonomy. Christ's kingdom is made up of those who are willing to lay down their lives—including their own success, privilege, and power—in love for others. We must be willing to give God our loyalty even above our religious traditions.

*Jesus, I'm so glad that you are better than the leaders of this world. I choose to follow you, my humble King.*

# Grounded Expectations

"Remember what I taught you, that a servant isn't superior to his master. And since they persecuted me, they will also persecute you. And if they obey my teachings, they will also obey yours."

JOHN 15:20

If we expect to live in this world unscathed by suffering, we are not grounded in the reality of what life requires of us. God does not destine us for suffering, but he certainly tells us to expect it. If Jesus did not escape the criticism of the leaders of his day, why would we expect to rise above such a thing?

The fact remains: we cannot please everyone. No matter how hard we try, some people won't like us. They won't like what we stand for or who we are. No amount of bending or shape-shifting will ever change this. It is not worth it to even try. When people persecute us, not because we have done something wrong but because of our love for Christ, we should not be surprised. What Jesus faced, so will we.

*Jesus, I'm so glad you gave realistic advice, wisdom, and expectations. It is a relief to know that pain is an unavoidable part of life. Thank you for being with me in my pain.*

## One and the Same

"If anyone hates me,
they hate my Father also."

JOHN 15:23

Jesus was a perfect representation of the Father on earth. Everything he did, the Father had done first. Everything he taught was given from the wisdom of the Father. Jesus did nothing on his own. He made this clear so that the religious leaders would not be fooled. If they had known the Father, they would have recognized Jesus. If they hated Jesus, it also meant that they hated the Father.

Many of the religious leaders of Jesus' day persecuted him. They hated him. Though they were experts of Jewish law, they completely missed the Messiah. If we are not careful, we can value our religious traditions and understanding more than we value the person of Christ. If we hold others to standards we feel we are above, then we should look more closely at our hearts. God is so forgiving and kind, and he restores those who come to him. Let's humble ourselves before him and allow his love to transform our mindsets.

*Lord Jesus, I love you—not just what I've been taught about you but you, the person of Christ. Your character is unbelievably good, true, and loving. Transform my thoughts in the power of your presence.*

## Divine Encouragement

"I will send you the Divine Encourager from the very presence of my Father. He will come to you, the Spirit of Truth, emanating from the Father, and he will speak to you about me."

JOHN 15:26

The Spirit of God is not only for our help but also for our encouragement. The Spirit of Truth comes straight from the presence of the Father. Meditate on this for a moment. The Spirit of God, the same one who makes his home in you, is simultaneously with the Father. What a word picture we are given in this verse: "The Spirit…*emanating* from the Father" (emphasis added). The Spirit of God radiates from his being.

Turn your attention to this Divine Encourager. Feel the warmth of his light that emits from the Father's face. He ushers you into the presence of God. He is the presence of God. God does not just give us guidelines to live by. He offers us himself. He gives us encouragement. He teaches us with his wisdom. He offers all the help we need. What a gloriously good God he is to us!

*Divine Encourager, thank you for offering me all that I could ever need or want in the fullness of your friendship. I am indebted to you.*

## Anchor of Truth

"I have told you this so that you would not surrender
to confusion or doubt."

JOHN 16:1

Jesus did not want his friends to be confused about what
was about to happen to him. He also didn't want them to
despair. Jesus graciously shared wisdom, insight, and warn-
ings so that they would not be caught off guard.

If we were to believe that life in Christ is easy, then at
the first sign of trouble, we would falter. We cannot avoid the
pangs of grief or the heavy weight of suffering. Jesus never
promised that we would escape these. We must remember
that the One who promised us his presence is faithful to
be with us through it all. The abundance of his life is ours
through fellowship with his Spirit. We get the peace of God,
the joy of God, and his love and hope in the midst of every
trial. This is the anchor of truth we can hold on to when the
going gets tough.

*Lord of Truth, thank you for not shying away from the hard
topics with your disciples. I am so grateful for your wisdom
and presence. I am thankful to have you through every hill
and valley of this life.*

## Something Better

> "Here's the truth: It's to your advantage that I go away, for if I don't go away the Divine Encourager will not be released to you. But after I depart, I will send him to you."
>
> JOHN 16:7

When Jesus walked this earth, he was confined to being in one place at a time. He let his divinity be encapsulated within flesh and bones, fully taking on the human experience. He could not be everywhere at once, as the Spirit can and does. Only after Jesus ascended to the Father's side was the Holy Spirit sent to fill God's people on Pentecost.

What a blessing it is for us to live in the time of the Spirit's presence poured out on all who look to Christ. He is not confined by any of us, and still he chooses to make his home in those who put their faith in Christ, the Son of God. The disciples did not realize at the time the tradeoff that would happen. Perhaps you have been dreading a transition that feels like a sort of death. Know this: out of every ending comes a new beginning. And with God, new beginnings are usually upgrades of encounter.

*Lord, thank you for always doing something new and bringing something beautiful out of the letting go. I trust you.*

## The Spirit's Work

"When he comes, he will expose sin and prove that the world is wrong about God's righteousness and his judgments."

JOHN 16:8

It is the Spirit's work to expose sin and prove that the world is wrong about God's righteousness and his judgments. It is not our job to judge others. It is ours to advocate for the poor and vulnerable ones in society. We don't have to seek favor from politicians or powerful people. There is no need to compromise our integrity in order to gain influence or to expose another. The Spirit does the work of God, and this includes the judgments of God.

We are called to love others well. This will always be true. The Spirit empowers us to do this by giving us grace to offer others. He moves within us, transforming our hearts and minds in the wisdom of Christ. Let's be sure we leave the Spirit's work to the Spirit and take up the work that God has given us. We are partners, but we are not micromanagers, and neither is God.

*Spirit, do what only you can do in people's hearts and turn them to you. Expose the sin in the world and prove what God's righteousness and judgments actually are.*

# A Little at a Time

> "There is so much more I would like to say to you,
> but it's more than you can grasp at this moment."
>
> JOHN 16:12

In his last teaching time with his disciples, Jesus wanted to share much more with them. He knew, however, that anything else would just go over their heads. He is a wise and patient teacher. Jesus did not finish guiding his friends even after his death. When the Holy Spirit was poured out upon them, he continued the work in each believer.

Why are we in a rush to understand more than we are able to at any given moment? Let's rest in the wisdom God offers us and trust that he will teach us more when we are ready to listen and learn. He is aware of our capacity, and we will not miss out on what he has for us as long as we keep spending time with him and seeking him. He continues to reveal himself in deeper wisdom as we sit at his feet.

*Jesus, you are so gracious with me. Thank you for the relief of knowing I will not miss what you have for me. I am your student, Lord. Continue to teach me all the days of my life.*

## Unveiled Truth

"When the truth-giving Spirit comes, he will unveil the reality of every truth within you. He won't speak on his own, but only what he hears from the Father, and he will reveal prophetically to you what is to come."

JOHN 16:13

God reveals the truth *within* us. He unveils our understanding as he teaches us deep within and imparts his wisdom to our minds and hearts. Have you ever had the experience of a sudden understanding of something you had not before realized? Perhaps it felt like a curtain being pulled back in your mind, and all at once, you knew what was hidden before.

This is the kind of truth unveiling that the Spirit can do in us. He gives us pictures, impressions, and words that are straight from the Father. He only speaks what is from the Father's heart. And how can we know that it is from God? We test the fruit of it, and we see whether it lines up with the nature of God and his already revealed Word. Ask and listen for the reality of truth you have not yet known and wait on God's response.

*Spirit of Truth, unveil revelations of God's glory in my heart, mind, and understanding. I worship you for all that you are.*

## New Ways of Knowing

"Soon you won't see me any longer, but then, after a little while, you will see me in a new way."

JOHN 16:16

The disciples believed that Jesus was the Son of God. Their expectations of the Messiah didn't include his being crucified even though Jesus warned them as clearly as he could that he would not be with them for much longer. They had to let their old expectations and ways of knowing die when Jesus did and leave the door open for new ways of knowing him.

As with most things, Jesus did this work. He revealed himself to them after he rose from the grave. He continued to meet with them, eat with them, and teach them at various times before he ascended to heaven. He promised them that the Spirit would come and be a better friend than they could anticipate, continuing to teach them and empower them in his ways. When things don't go as we expect, we can make room for God to meet us in a new way. He is ever so faithful to do it.

*Jesus, thank you for your continued and faithful teaching, love, and direction. I am open to you, no matter how you come. Simply don't leave me alone in my disappointment.*

# Straight to the Father

"Here is eternal truth: When that time comes you won't need to ask me for anything, but instead you will go directly to the Father and ask him for anything you desire and he will give it to you, because of your relationship with me."

JOHN 16:23

Jesus acted as a mediator between his followers and God. This was not a foreign concept to the Jewish people. It was common for a high priest to present the offerings of the people to God on their behalf. Jesus promised a better way when the Spirit was poured out. Instead of going through someone else to relate and talk to God, it would be possible to go straight to the Father through relationship with the Son.

Do you rely on the spiritual practices of your leaders to make you right with God? Do you trust their relationship with him more than your own? Anyone who is in Christ is a new person, as 2 Corinthians 5:17 tells us. When we turn to God, he reconciles us to himself. We can go boldly before the Father's throne without waiting on anyone else. Jesus has opened the door and paved the way for us already.

*Father, I come freely and boldly to where love is enthroned. Fill me with your grace and align my heart with yours. I love you.*

## Time to Ask

"Until now you've not been bold enough to ask the Father for a single thing in my name, but now you can ask, and keep on asking him! And you can be sure that you'll receive what you ask for, and your joy will have no limits!"

JOHN 16:24

Jesus gives us permission to ask the Father to move in our lives through the authority of his name. Keep on asking, Jesus said. When we are aligned with Christ, he transforms our hearts in his living love. His desires become important to us. His ways inform our understanding of what he would do in this world. With confidence, we can ask for the things that are on Jesus' heart. With boldness, we can ask for these things in Jesus' name.

When was the last time you asked the Father for something in Jesus' name? What kind of a request was it? Don't worry about getting it wrong. Know that the Father meets you with kindness, patience, and mercy. Keep pressing in to knowing Christ more through his Word and through fellowship with his Spirit. The more you get to know him, the more confident you will become in using his name, for your requests will reflect his nature and heart.

*Lord, I trust that I don't have to ask perfectly to be heard by you. I will keep on asking, knowing you hear me and read my heart so well.*

# In the Father's Presence

"I came to you sent from the Father's presence,
and I entered into the created world,
and now I will leave this world and return to the Father's side."

JOHN 16:28

Jesus came from the Father's presence, and it's to his presence he would return. Full circle, he completed the purpose of his mission. He revealed the Father's heart to a world hungry to know the truth of who he is. He revealed the incomparable mercy of God that religious institutions had watered down. He came to set the sinner free, to heal the sick, and to conquer the power of death. Everything he did was in the Father's heart for him to do.

We have no further to look than the life of Christ to get a handle on who the Father is, what he is like, and what he wants to do in and for us. The Father doesn't seek to steal, kill, or destroy. That is the reputation of the enemy. If our idea of God does not align with the compassionate truth of Christ, then we must be willing to change our minds about him.

*Jesus, thank you for revealing the powerful love of the Father through your life and ministry. Transform my understanding of God's motives and heart in light of your great love.*

# Completely Convinced

"Now we understand that you know everything there is to know, and we don't need to question you further. And everything you've taught us convinces us that you have come directly from God!"

JOHN 16:30

The disciples were grateful for clear, unveiled speech from their beloved teacher and friend. They could at last understand what before seemed like a riddle. Jesus had used parables, analogies, and figurative speech to teach his many followers throughout his ministry, but in his last talk with his disciples, he laid all of those aside.

Have you ever been completely convinced of the lordship of Christ? What was it that won over your faith? Perhaps you have believed, but a part of you still feels unsure. Christ takes our little bit of faith and marries it to his faithfulness. He will never stop being loyal to his nature. He cannot change, and that is really good news. Whether or not you are fully convinced of who God is today, you can come to him with curiosity, seeds of faith, and a humble heart. He can grow gardens of glory with your surrendered heart.

*Jesus, there are times when I don't question who you are and others when I struggle to believe the fullness of your love. Even still, I am yours.*

# Conqueror of the World

"Everything I've taught you is so that the peace which is in me will be in you and will give you great confidence as you rest in me. For in this unbelieving world you will experience trouble and sorrows, but you must be courageous, for I have conquered the world!"

JOHN 16:33

What an invitation Christ offers us! His teachings lead us to rivers of peace that offer confidence and rest. Even when we experience trouble and sorrows, this pervasive peace is our portion. Courage keeps us going. It keeps us pushing into the presence of God as we face our hardest days. Even in these dark times, we can have the great confidence of Christ's peace that brings us deep soul rest.

Jesus has conquered the world—all its temptations, sufferings, and sorrows. He has gone through the range of human experience and emotion. He was subject to the limitations of his humanity, and yet he overcame the power of sin and death. He chose to love in the face of persecution. He chose to heal in the face of naysayers. He chose to humble himself in great courage, purpose, and passion. In the end, he overcame what we could never overcome on our own. What a wonderful and powerful Savior!

*Jesus, fill me with your peace that passes understanding and give me courage to keep following after you.*

# Prayer of Alignment

This is what Jesus prayed as he looked up into heaven,
"Father, the time has come. Unveil the glorious splendor of your
Son so that I will magnify your glory!"

JOHN 17:1

Jesus, having said all that he could to his disciples and knowing that the time of his arrest and death was approaching, launched into a prayer to his Father. The time had come, and Jesus prayed that the Father would unveil his splendor through him. Everything Jesus did was to bring the Father glory. There was no competition, only complete and total unity.

Whose glory are you living for? Are you seeking the accolades and attention of other people or the integrity of your own soul? When you are overly focused on pleasing people, you may miss out on the things that truly bring you alive, bring you purpose, and allow for a deep sense of presiding peace. Jesus knew who he was, why he was sent, and the power of his sacrifice. Ask the Lord to help you focus on these things if you are struggling in this regard. Then, when your time has come, you may join with his prayer that the Father's glory would be magnified through your life.

*Father, I want to live with the satisfaction of being true to who you've created me to be. Help me realign with that purpose. Thank you.*

## Authority over All

"You have already given me authority over all people so that I may give the gift of eternal life to all those that you have given to me."

JOHN 17:2

Jesus' responsibility and authority extend to all people. Not one of us is outside of his jurisdiction. When we embrace Christ, he gives us the gift of eternal life. This is an overwhelming and glorious gift! When we yield our lives to him, we do not have to wonder about his heart toward us. His mercy-kindness is great, and it covers our sin. When we wield this same love in our relationships with others, "love will be a canopy over a multitude of sins" (1 Peter 4:8). As God does toward us, so we get to practice with others.

Jesus is Lord over all. This truth is plainly laid out for us in Philippians 2:10: "The authority of the name of Jesus causes every knee to bow in reverence! Everything and everyone will one day submit to this name." If we are discouraged by the world around us, let's put our hope in Christ, who promises to set all wrong things right in his name and in his time. What he has promised, he will do.

*Jesus, I bow under your authority and trust your timing. I know you will not fail to follow through on your Word.*

# Restored to Glory

"My Father, restore me back to the glory that we shared together
when we were face-to-face before the universe was created."

JOHN 17:5

Jesus is the divine image of God. "For God, who said, 'Let brilliant light shine out of darkness,' is the one who has cascaded his light into us—the brilliant dawning light of the glorious knowledge of God as we gaze into the face of Jesus Christ" (2 Corinthians 4:6). The glory of God is evident when we fellowship with Christ through his Spirit. We do not yet see the Lord face-to-face, and yet we can see him with the eyes of our hearts.

The Glorious One is already in his rightful place with the Father. It is our honor to search out the glory of God through his living Word. "God conceals the revelation of his word in the hiding place of his glory. But the honor of kings is revealed by how they thoroughly search out the deeper meaning of all that God says" (Proverbs 25:2). Let's not hold back our search of God, for he reveals himself to those who seek him with all their hearts.

*Lord, thank you for revealing your glory through the revelation of your living Word and presence. I want to know you and worship you in spirit and in truth.*

# Manifestation of the Father

*"Father, I have manifested who you really are and I have revealed you to the men and women that you gave to me. They were yours, and you gave them to me, and they have fastened your Word firmly to their hearts."*

JOHN 17:6

Jesus made the character of the Father visible to his followers. He acted in the same way the Father would. Jesus' character *is* the character of God. His mercy, his justice, and his patience all reflect those in the heart of God. His wisdom, grace, and power are the revelation of the Father's own characteristics. If you wonder whether the Father is gracious, compassionate, caring, and kind, look at the life of Jesus. What you find in him is the evidence of God's nature.

If we want to display the nature of God in our own lives, we must follow Jesus' commands. His law of love is not a suggestion; it is the very heart and standard of God. His humble kindness and steadfast truth reveal that there is no self-promotion in the kingdom of heaven, but there is confidence and conviction. May we follow his example, pressing in to know him through fellowship with his Spirit. The more we know him, the more like him we can become.

*Jesus Christ, thank you for revealing the true character of God. You are not easily angered though you do burn with passion for justice. You are wonderful, and it is my honor to live for you.*

## Carry the Word

> "The very words you gave to me to speak I have passed on to them. They have received your words and carry them in their hearts. They are convinced that I have come from your presence, and they have fully believed that you sent me to represent you."
>
> JOHN 17:8

Just as Jesus carried the words of God and passed them on to his followers, so can we carry the words of Christ in our hearts. We must value the wisdom he offers us, for it is more precious than the treasures of this world. It is more costly than gold and precious stones. As Proverbs 3:13–14 says, "Blessings pour over the ones who find wisdom, for they have obtained living-understanding. As wisdom increases, a great treasure is imparted, greater than many bars of refined gold."

Through Christ, we have invaluable wisdom. As we receive his instruction and carry his Word within our hearts, the treasures of God are imparted to us. This cannot be over-stated: the wisdom of God "is a more valuable commodity than gold and gemstones, for there is nothing you desire that could compare to her" (v. 15). Let the wisdom of God lead you deeper into the glory of God, and carry this treasure in your heart.

*Word of God, you are the wisdom of God made manifest. I delight in receiving you, living for you, and coming alive in you.*

## *Deep Love*

"With deep love, I pray for my disciples. I'm not asking on behalf of the unbelieving world, but for those who belong to you, those you have given me."

JOHN 17:9

Jesus prayed for those he loved. He prayed for his friends and followers, those who proved their loyalty to him. Though he loves everyone, his disciples held a deep and precious place in his heart. They were his companions those three years of ministry, leaving their lives behind to know him. They were precious to him, and he did not neglect to pray specifically for their lives.

Isn't it the same with us? Don't we pray for those we dearly love with a fervor that cannot be matched when we pray for strangers? We were built for deep connection and intimate friendship. Even Jesus had his chosen few whom he would retreat away with. It is not wise to be deeply vulnerable with all people. True and deep connection takes time, but it is worth it. May we follow the lead of Jesus in being selective about those to whom we emotionally bare ourselves. Loving friendship built with bridges of trust is a beautiful gift.

*Jesus, thank you for your example. Help me to balance vulnerability and trust with those who are invested in me and I in them.*

## Glory in Surrender

"All who belong to me now belong to you. And all who belong to you now belong to me as well, and my glory is revealed through their surrendered lives."

JOHN 17:10

If we truly want to reveal the glory of God through our lives, we cannot overlook the importance of surrender. Paul said it this way in Galatians 2:20: "My old identity has been co-crucified with Christ and no longer lives...for the Anointed One lives his life through me—we live in union as one!" Faith in the Son of God empowers our new lives, for Christ dispenses his life into ours.

A vessel that is closed cannot receive what is being poured out. If we want to be filled with the glory of God, we must open ourselves to him, and this requires surrender to the Son of God. As long as we hold tightly to our own lives, we may miss out on the possibilities of God's plans and purposes through us. "We are to live as those who live in the world but are not absorbed by it, for the world as we know it is quickly passing away" (1 Corinthians 7:31). The kingdom of eternity will never lose its power, so let's live for the glory of God in surrender to his ways.

*Jesus, I yield to you and your kingdom. You are better than my understanding.*

## Protection in Unity

"Holy Father, I am about to leave this world to return and be with you, but my disciples will remain here. Holy Father, each one that you have given me, keep them in your name so that they will be united as one, even as we are one."

JOHN 17:11

Have you ever experienced someone you respect and look up to moving on to something else while you stayed behind? It could be in ministry or in a job setting. It could be the death of someone you loved. For those left behind in the wake of someone else's leaving, their resolve will be tested. Unity with the person who has left will either strengthen or dissolve, depending on how intentionally we work to stay connected.

God wants us unified in love. We know that no person, organization, or family does this perfectly. Perfection is not the end goal: lived-out love is. Jesus prayed for his disciples to be protected and unified in purpose. In order to do this, the disciples would need to remain focused on the teachings Jesus instilled in them. They would need to remember his example. They would need to remember their primary purpose. The same is true for us.

*Jesus, unify your people in love. I humble my heart before you and remember the purpose to which you have called me. Thank you.*

# *Waterfall of Delight*

"I am returning to you so Father, I pray that they will experience and enter into my joyous delight in you so that it is fulfilled in them and overflows."

JOHN 17:13

Jesus does not simply say, "Follow me," and then tell us to fall into line or else. There is joy in the presence of God. David declared, "Because of you, I know the path of life, as I taste the fullness of joy in your presence. At your right side I experience divine pleasures forevermore!" (Psalm 16:11). This is not a fleeting happiness that David spoke of, and it is not what Jesus meant either. It is divine pleasures.

David also prophesied about Christ in the following way: "You have revealed to me the pathways to life, and seeing your face fills me with euphoria" (Acts 2:28). Seeing the Father filled Jesus with joyous delight, and we are invited to share in this blissful experience as we look to him. He is pure love, radiating the glory of God. There is no darkness hidden in him. He is the fullness of peace, joy, love, hope, and light. He is the abundance of life that we long for.

*Shining One, rain over me with the deluge of your delight. Refresh me in your living waters of pure peace. You are the one I love.*

## *Loyal to Love's Ways*

"I have given them your message and that is why the unbelieving world hates them. For their allegiance is no longer to this world because I am not of this world."

JOHN 17:14

The world hates what it cannot control. Those who live under Love's leadership do not bow to the whims of power and prestige. They do not give in to the compromises of manipulation, lying, or cheating. They cannot be manipulated by a system that requires blind allegiance. Love liberates us from the need to fit in. We can live courageously in line with the value system of God, which finds no excuse for abuse, arrogance, or hatred.

Take a look at your life. Consider what the fruit of it displays. What have you given your allegiance to? Really reflect on whether the causes you align yourself with demonstrate the love of Christ. His truth is unwavering, and it is always laced with mercy. Beware of the things that take away the honor of humility and mercy-kindness. Align yourself with Christ's values, and you will be free of the allegiance to systems of this world.

*Merciful Christ, open my eyes to see where I have been aligning with people, systems, and ideologies that come against your values. I humble myself under your love's law.*

# Guarded from Evil

"I am not asking that you remove them from the world, but I ask that you guard their hearts from evil, for they no longer belong to this world any more than I do."

JOHN 17:15–16

Jesus said, "Your lives light up the world. For how can you hide a city that stands on a hilltop?" (Matthew 5:14). We are not meant to retreat from the world but to be living lights in it. This is why Christ prayed that his disciples would be protected. He asked that the Father would guard their hearts from evil, for their true home was with the Father and the Son in their forever kingdom.

It is the Father's work through the Spirit that guards our hearts against evil. As we submit to his leadership, he lovingly corrects us when we go off course. Then we can truly heed the advice of Jesus, who said, "Don't hide your light! Let it shine brightly before others, so that your commendable works will shine as light upon them, and then they will give their praise to your Father in heaven" (v. 16).

*Father, guard my heart in your love and correct me when I am getting it wrong. I submit to your leadership today and every day. I am yours.*

# Dedicated Holy Sacrifice

"I dedicate myself to them as a holy sacrifice so that they will live as fully dedicated to God and be made holy by your truth."

JOHN 17:19

Jesus' dedication of his life as a holy sacrifice on the behalf of his disciples is a beautiful testament to the power of what he offers each of us who believe in him. He is our holiness. His sacrifice allows us to live as fully dedicated to God because it is this very sacrifice that makes us right with God. "Through his powerful declaration of acquittal, God freely gives away his righteousness…all because Jesus, the Anointed One, has liberated us from the guilt, punishment, and power of sin" (Romans 3:24).

Even though we all sin and are in need of the glory of God, the way has already been paved. Jesus Christ is our righteousness. The free gift of salvation is offered through faith in him. The faithfulness of Christ is our guarantee. What a glorious gift and reality! What a worthy Savior he is of all our devotion!

*Anointed One, thank you for becoming our righteousness and for offering yourself on our behalf. May my life reflect your love as I live for you.*

# Jesus' Prayer for You

"I ask not only for these disciples, but also for all those who will one day believe in me through their message."

JOHN 17:20

Before Jesus went to the cross, he took time to pray *for you*. Any who believe in Christ through the message of the disciples (through the Scriptures of the New Testament) are included in this prayer. The testimony of Christ has reached through history to reach you through their message.

Jesus looked with hope through time, and he made it a priority to pray for you and me. This same thoughtful Christ still prays for us before the Father. Romans 8:34 posits the question, "How could he possibly condemn us since he is continually praying for our triumph?" He is our divine intercessor, praying for our victory. His love reaches us today, and no small bit of it either. The "demonstrated love [of God] is our glorious victory over everything" (v. 37).

*Jesus, thank you for interceding on my behalf, both back then and even now. Your love empowers me to overcome this world. Your fierce mercy does not relent, and it won't ever fail. Thank you.*

## Passionate Love

"You live fully in me and now I live fully in them so that they will experience perfect unity, and the world will be convinced that you have sent me, for they will see that you love each one of them with the same passionate love that you have for me."

JOHN 17:23

We can find perfect unity in the passionate love of Christ. As we see Jesus in one another, we can more readily ground our opinions of ourselves in our shared humanity and the grace of God. The passionate love of the Father toward Christ is the same fervent love God has for us.

When we look through the lens of God's outrageous love, we see people the way that God does. His compassion compelled him to send Christ, and Christ is the fullness of our salvation. We come to the Father through him, and we dwell in the love that was from the beginning overflowing toward all that he made. This love is a raging river, never ebbing, always flowing. May we follow its tide as we interact with others today.

*Lord, thank you for the power of your love that overcomes every bias, breaks down every barrier, and opens up every possibility for goodness. I yield to your passionate love and allow you to move me where you will.*

## *Perfection of Knowing*

"Father, I ask that you allow everyone that you have given to me to be with me where I am! Then they will see my full glory—the very splendor you have placed upon me because you have loved me even before the beginning of time."

JOHN 17:24

The life we are called to live in Christ is a life of faith. But this does not mean that we have no glimpses of God's glory. His faithfulness fuels our faith to take us deeper into dependency on his love. Yes, we will see the fullness of Christ's glory after we die. This is true! Still, Ephesians 2:6 says, "He raised us up with Christ the exalted One, and we ascended with him into the glorious perfection and authority of the heavenly realm, for we are now co-seated as one with Christ!"

If we are *now* co-seated with Christ in heavenly places, that means that we have access to this perfection of knowing him. We wait, and yet we don't have to wait. We long, and yet our longings are being fulfilled. What a mystery this is—fellowship with God! For all that we taste and see now, there is so much more for us to discover in the wonders of his glorious presence.

*Jesus Christ, you are glorified and lifted high right now. I worship you as such. You are my Lord, my King, and my Leader. Reveal yourself to me in new ways as I look to you.*

## Even More Real

> "I have revealed to them who you are and I will continue to make
> you even more real to them, so that they may experience the
> same endless love that you have for me, for your love will now live
> in them, even as I live in them!"
>
> JOHN 17:26

Jesus' gracious offering to us is that he will continue to reveal the reality of God to us. How wonderfully generous! He revealed the Father through his time on earth, but that was not enough. He promised to continue to unveil the reality of the Father through the indwelling of his Spirit. It is through a living relationship with Christ that we uncover how wonderfully good God is, and this is a never-ending journey for us.

All that you know about God is a starting point. The truth of his love revealed to you is a wonderful gift that keeps on giving. Don't neglect the access you have to God through his love living within you. There is more to discover in him today. The Glorious One is alive in you.

*God, thank you for the nearness of your love and for the power of your presence. Become even more real to me today.*

## The Garden

After Jesus finished this prayer; he left with his disciples and went across the Kidron Valley to a place where there was a garden.

JOHN 18:1

I don't know about you, but I love a garden. Close to nature, the nurtured blooms, and the whispering trees, I feel close to God. Perhaps Jesus felt this way too. In a place of peace, Jesus would pour out his anguish. He went to this garden—what we know as the garden of Gethsemane—in order to wait for his captors. This was the garden of his betrayal, and even there, Jesus stood faithful.

When life is tough, where do you retreat? Perhaps you go to the mountains or the sea. Maybe you find a quiet place within your home. May the faithfulness of God find you as you retreat from the world. May his peace wrap around you no matter what you face when you return. He is near, he is loyal, and he will not abandon you in the time of your great need.

*Jesus, thank you for meeting with me as I retreat from the stresses of life and even when I can't get away from them. I am grateful for your persistent presence.*

## Unnecessary Force

> The Pharisees and the leading priests had given Judas a large detachment of Roman soldiers and temple police to seize Jesus. Judas guided them to the garden, all of them carrying torches and lanterns and armed with swords and spears.
>
> JOHN 18:3

With the number of weapons the guards brought with them to arrest Jesus, you would think he was a violent threat to all of them. We know, however, that Jesus did not put up a fight. This was yet another way he demonstrated the mercy of God. Had it not been his time, he wouldn't have fought them then either. He would have slipped away, just as he had numerous times before.

Jesus, our great and mighty peacemaker, willingly laid down his life for us. We should also not hold so tightly to our rights that we miss the opportunity to display the mercy of Christ. We need not use violence to put up a fight. In fact, violence is not the way of the kingdom of God. In Matthew 5:39 Jesus said, "Don't repay an evil act with another evil act." May we remember his words and the values of his mercy and peace when we are tempted to lash out at others.

*Jesus, no one could take your life away from you without you willingly laying it down. May I follow in your footsteps, refusing to cut down or demean another, especially not in your name.*

## Powerful Identity

"Jesus of Nazareth," they replied. (Now Judas, the traitor, was among them.) He replied, "I am he." And the moment Jesus spoke the words, "I am he," the mob fell backward to the ground!

JOHN 18:5–6

At the power of his voice and declaration, the mob seeking to take Jesus captive fell to the ground. Imagine this scene. Jesus simply announced who he was (though the announcement he made was his identity: I AM he). Jesus offered himself up, not wasting any time. But he also clearly displayed his power.

What a stunning event this was for all in attendance! Both his disciples and his captors witnessed the power of his name. Jesus, knowing he was in charge of how this would go, permitted the guards to seize him. He submitted himself to cruelty even though he did not deserve it in the least. What a wonderful Savior! Is there anything you've been withholding from him? Consider surrendering it to him today, for he is fully God and fully loving toward you. You can trust him.

*Christ Jesus, you displayed your power and authority in the garden, and still you surrendered to the cruelty of those men. What juxtaposition! I trust you with my life, Lord.*

# Put Away Your Sword

Suddenly, Peter took out his sword and struck the high priest's servant, slashing off his right ear! The servant's name was Malchus. Jesus ordered Peter, "Put your sword away! Do you really think I will avoid the suffering which my Father has assigned to me?"

JOHN 18:10–11

When others incite violence, Christ says that we should lay down our weapons. Peter took out his sword to defend his Savior. His heart was in the right place. He did not yet understand all that Christ had taught about laying down one's life in love though. Even so, our Savior deals with the realities of our shortcomings. He instructs us and corrects us in kindness.

Jesus showed kindness to both the captor and his friend when he healed one and corrected the other. Jesus reassured his friend; this was part of the Father's assignment for him. Have you ever thought you knew better than a friend when their response was not what you expected? We can see both Peter and Jesus in this conundrum, yet one was the divine response, and the other was self-protective. Let's surrender under the leadership of Christ and allow his perspective and mercy to correct us even when we think we are doing the right thing.

*Jesus, I lay down my weapons and trust you to do more in mercy than I could with force. Your ways are better.*

## Disappointing Denial

As he passed inside, the young servant girl guarding the gate took
a look at Peter and said to him, "Aren't you one of his disciples?"
He denied it, saying, "No! I'm not!"

JOHN 18:17

Jesus had predicted Peter's denial, yet Peter hadn't believed
him at the time. His self-righteousness kept him from
accepting the possibility of his own weakness in the face
of tremendous pressure and threat. The disappointment in
Peter's denial was less on the side of his Savior and more
within Peter himself, who thought he was above such things.

Frankly, it did not matter whether Peter believed himself
to be capable of denying his friend and teacher. The result of
his actions said it all. When was the last time you felt deeply
disappointed in yourself? None of us can escape our failures.
None of us is perfect. It is how we respond after we fail that
sets us on the path either to restoration or destruction. Our
Savior knows us and forgives us quickly. We must also learn
to forgive ourselves.

*Jesus, I don't want to project my own disappointment with
myself onto you. You are kind, gracious, and so forgiving. Help
me to learn to be the same, even with myself. Thank you.*

## Nothing to Hide

Jesus answered Annas' questions by saying, "I have said nothing in secret. At all times I have taught openly and publicly in a synagogue, in the temple courts, and wherever the people assemble."

JOHN 18:20

Jesus had absolutely nothing to hide as he stood before the high priest under interrogation. He had openly taught the people, having said nothing in secret to incriminate himself. His ministry was open and in public for all who wanted to listen.

Have you ever been under attack for a baseless accusation? When you walk in the light of integrity, what others presume about you is not your business. You have only to keep living as you ought in the integrity of your values and love's power over your life. Do not be intimidated by the threats of others. Even when they succeed in convincing others of their assumptions, God knows your heart, and he knows the truth. Let that be your confidence and continue on with nothing to hide.

*Jesus, you know me better than anyone else knows me. I know I am not perfect, but I want to live with integrity. Help me to stand strong even in the face of false accusations.*

## Witnesses of Truth

"Why would you ask me for evidence to condemn me?
Ask those who have heard what I've taught.
They can tell you."

JOHN 18:21

The testimony of eyewitnesses is an important tool in the hands of either a defender or a prosecutor. Jesus testified about himself freely, and he acted in powerful ways that displayed the mercy of God. There were many witnesses of his miracles. Many people, religious leaders included, also listened to his wise teachings.

Though we may talk about ideologies all day long, there is power in being a witness. A lived experience holds weight that is far greater than second-hand information. We each are witnesses of God's truth through our lived experiences. We have the Spirit of God alive and moving in our midst. When we witness the power of God at work coupled with the wisdom and perfection of Christ's mercy, we become partakers of God's truth.

*Jesus, thank you for the power of your love that I've been a witness to. Your ways are perfect, and you continue to move in mighty acts of miracle mercy. Thank you.*

## Unjust Abuse

Jesus replied, "If my words are evil, then prove it.
But if I haven't broken any laws, then why would you hit me?"

JOHN 18:23

Without proof of any wrongdoing, the Sanhedrin and the temple guards abused Jesus. Perhaps you know this type of abuse yourself, or you know someone who has gone through unjust suffering. Jesus knows your pain. He knows it all too well. Take comfort in the arms of your Savior. He not only cares for you but also understands what you have been through. He took the unfounded accusations against him and was beaten, bloodied, and bruised. It is never his heart or purpose for anyone to undergo such horrific suffering, especially innocent ones.

Maybe you know someone who has let the pain of their past keep them from embracing the love of Christ now. Perhaps they need to know that their Savior knows what unjust suffering feels like. They can find solace in the heart of God, and they can also find healing. Their overcoming victory is found not in pulling up their bootstraps but by being loved to life in the mercy of Christ's fellowship.

*Savior, the fact that you were unjustly abused and suffered for crimes you did not commit does not sit lightly with me. Yet it brings me closer to you to know that you know such pain and that you offer me your overcoming victory.*

# He Knows Our Weakness

Peter denied it the third time and said, "No!"—and at that very same moment, a rooster crowed nearby.

JOHN 18:27

It wasn't until he had denied Christ for the third time and the rooster crowed that Peter remembered what Jesus had told him at the Passover meal. Jesus knew that Peter would deny him. It was grace that alerted Peter to this fact, even though he couldn't entertain the possibility. At that moment, when the rooster crowed, Peter remembered. Matthew 26:75 recounts that "with a shattered heart, Peter left the courtyard, sobbing with bitter tears."

Jesus is not surprised by our failures, though we may very well be. How can we disappoint him when he knows what we are capable of? His mercy is strong enough to know our weaknesses and offer us grace to forgive us, restore us, and embrace us. If you have struggled to get back to where you were after a personal failure, know this: God is ready to restore you in kindness. Turn to him.

*Merciful Jesus, thank you for not condemning me even when you know what I am capable of. Your love is stronger than my failure, and you restore me with grace every time I return to you. Thank you.*

## Empty Accusations

Pilate came outside where they waited and asked them pointedly, "Tell me, what exactly is the accusation that you bring against this man? What has he done?"

JOHN 18:29

It is important to know when our hearts are turned against someone. What do we have against them? The answer to that question reveals a lot about our character and perhaps a bit of our history with hurt. Jesus did not deserve the punishment he received. He was not guilty of bringing harm. He was the one who offered abundant life, restoring limbs and raising dead bodies. He offered a way for us to know the Father and to truly recognize his love for us.

The anger of many of the religious leaders who, frankly, were threatened by Jesus' influence and who wanted to hold on to their own authority, led them to hurl accusations at Jesus. Little did they know, however, that in his dying, Christ would set the world free. Let's be wary of our own biases and be sure to question our motives when we have darts of accusation at the ready.

*Savior, I don't want to be a modern-day denier of your power and lordship. I humble my heart before you. Cover me in your lavish love and reveal the seeds of bitterness that I need to remove from my heart.*

## *Looking for a Reason*

Pilate responded, "Only a Jew would care about this;
do I look like a Jew? It's your own people and your religious
leaders that have handed you over to me. So tell me,
Jesus, what have you done wrong?"

JOHN 18:35

Pilate was an outsider when it came to Jewish religious law. He was the governmental authority in the region, placed in Judea by the Romans. He had authority to sentence a criminal to death. First, though, Pilate was curious. What had Jesus done wrong?

The fact that Jesus' own people and religious leaders had handed him over to Pilate meant one thing: they wanted blood. If the matter could not be settled within the jurisdiction of their religious law, then it was because Jesus was a threat. Or so that's what Pilate thought. When we look for a reason to hate others, we will find it, though it may not be enough to stand up to an outsider's scrutiny. When we look for reasons to love others, we will also find them. May we do far more of the latter.

*Jesus, I don't want to be like those who look for reasons to support their bent toward hatred. I don't want to be self-serving and protect my biases. I want to know you and to live in the truth. Soften my heart in your love.*

# *Power from Another Realm*

Jesus looked at Pilate and said, "The royal power of my kingdom realm doesn't come from this world. If it did, then my followers would be fighting to the end to defend me from the Jewish leaders. My kingdom realm authority is not from this realm."

JOHN 18:36

The power of Christ's reign is not found in the halls of human palaces. It cannot be contained by the limits of the world's laws. His power is from another realm, the realm that was, is, and always will be. It is this greater authority that raised Christ from the grave three days after he was laid in it. It is this power that cancelled the curse of sin over our souls. It is this influence that promises we will one day rise up to be with him as well.

What authority are you living under in this world? Which kingdom has your allegiance? If it is to country, it is time to rethink your priorities. The kingdom of God does not belong to any one nation, not even solely to the Israelites. The kingdom of God is the eternal realm of Christ's reign. There will be representatives from every tribe, nation, and language. Every single one! Let's unite under the leadership of our loving King.

*King Jesus, I bow my knee to you, Lord. You are my ruler, and in you, all are welcome.*

### *Lovers of Truth*

Pilate responded, "Oh, so then you are a king?" "You are right."
Jesus said, "I was born a King, and I have come into this world to
prove what truth really is. And everyone who loves the truth will
receive my words."

JOHN 18:37

Let the power of what Christ said sink in: "I have come into this world to prove what truth really is." If we love truth, there is no way around it: we must embrace Christ. He revealed the truth of God's mercy, of his standards for justice, and of the invitation for all to freely come to the Father through him. The truth we are looking for is a person. It is Christ.

If we love truth, we will receive Jesus' words. Interestingly, the experts of the Torah were the very ones who rejected Christ. They thought they knew the truth already, but they completely missed it when it was embodied before them. Arrogance and pride do not account for love of truth. They prove love of self, influence, power, and prestige. Jesus is the Way, the Truth, and the Life. We must humble ourselves before him to receive the power of his life.

*Truth Speaker, I yield to your ways. I am a disciple of your truth. Teach me and correct me. I am your willing and humble student.*

# Not Even One Fault

Pilate looked at Jesus and said, "What is truth?" As silence filled the room, Pilate went back out to where the Jewish leaders were waiting and said to them, "He's not guilty. I couldn't even find one fault with him."

JOHN 18:38

Even as Pilate questioned what truth was, he could not deny the innocence of Jesus. He found nothing wrong with him, not even one fault. Legally and with a clean conscience, Pilate could not accuse this man.

This could have been the end of Jesus' abuse. Pilate could have freed him right then and there, but the people gathered before Pilate would not even hear of it. Their hearts were filled with such bitterness that they could not think clearly. Resentment and hostility never lead to good things. Cold hearts are not open to hearing a view that they don't agree with. May we not condemn those among us who are blameless, giving in to the pressure of the crowds around us. May we stand in truth and in solidarity with those whom the world is quick to condemn.

*Jesus, give me conviction and courage to stand with the innocent and hurting. I don't want to be a voice of condemnation that I will one day regret. Help me, Lord.*

## *Foolish Choices*

"You do know that we have a custom that I release one prisoner every year at Passover—shall I release your king—the king of the Jews?" They shouted out over and over, "No, not him! Give us Barabbas!" (Now Barabbas was a robber and a troublemaker.)

JOHN 18:39–40

Barabbas was no innocent man. He was a known troublemaker. The terms used for *robber* in both the Greek and Aramaic can also mean "one who leads an insurrection." That this kind of man was pitted against Jesus, who healed diseases and fed thousands of hungry followers, is laughable. It makes no sense at all that the Jewish leaders wanted a violent criminal released instead of Jesus.

Yes, we know that Christ willingly went through all of this. He knew what would happen. He knew what was in the hearts of humans and what they were capable of. And still, it doesn't make any of it right. It doesn't excuse any of it. It is important to be able to hold the weight of the nasty reality while also recognizing God's incredible grace and kindness in using this as an opportunity to overcome sin and death once and for all. Even though Christ does not condone these sorts of things, God can use even our worst life experiences and sow his mercy into the story. What a gracious God!

*God, thank you for your powerful and overwhelming grace. I am in awe of you.*

# Chance for Change

Once more Pilate went out and said to the Jewish officials, "I will bring him out once more so that you know that I've found nothing wrong with him."

JOHN 19:4

Sometimes in life, we get a chance to change our minds, an opportunity to weigh the truth and redirect our course of action. Whether we take advantage of that opportunity or not is up to us. It is good to take that pause and reevaluate. The Jewish officials had already made up their minds to get rid of Jesus. There was no turning back for them.

Even a hint of humility can open the door to mercy. May we lean toward the light of Christ that offers grace instead of doubling down on our stances that judge harshly. When there are opportunities to really evaluate our decisions, we should take them. Let's be sure to align our choices in the love and truth of Christ, our beautiful Savior.

*Jesus, may my heart remain soft in your love, bending to your mercy rather than to my own biases and preferences. Thank you for the chances you give me to realign in your kingdom ways.*

## Not Guilty

No sooner did the high priests and the temple guards see Jesus that they all shouted in a frenzy, "Crucify him! Crucify him!" Pilate replied, "You take him then and nail him to a cross yourselves! I told you—he's not guilty! I find no reason to condemn him."

JOHN 19:6

Though Pilate was not a man known for mercy, he initially refused to indict Jesus on baseless charges. It was only under pressure from the Jewish authorities, who claimed Pilate was no friend of Caesar if he let Jesus go, that Pilate relented. When we see an innocent life being abused and falsely accused, how easily do we fold under pressure? Will we truly stand for justice, predicated on our convictions and integrity, or will we give in to the manipulation and threats of others?

Integrity matters for all of us. If we have any position of power or influence, it is even more important that we love truth, mercy, and justice. May we, as followers of Christ, be known for our judicious and merciful ways, and may we not love our lives more than we love the truth. Integrity is a safeguard for those who live by its standards. Be true and refuse to condemn those who are not guilty.

*Jesus, even though there was nothing in you to condemn, you were still sentenced to death. This was an injustice, and yet you used it in ways that completely overpowered the evil meant toward you. Thank you.*

## Passover Lamb

> It was now almost noon. And it was the same day they were preparing to slay the Passover lambs. Then Pilate said to the Jewish officials, "Look! Here is your king!"
>
> JOHN 19:14

Even though Pilate's remark was probably not a serious one, it bears the weight of truth. Jesus, Israel's Messiah and King, appeared not as a governmental authority at the time but as the lamb who would be slain for their sins. He was their King even though they refused to believe. He was also their Passover Lamb.

Nothing that God does is without meaning. Everything came together to reveal the identity of Christ as Messiah. Though many could not accept this and refused to believe at the time, we see how true this was through the details of all that worked together. The Messiah, the Passover Lamb provided by God, paid the ultimate price for the sins of all people, the final price. There would never be a need for another sacrifice, for he paid the debt in full. Glory to God!

*Lamb of God, the power of your sacrifice cannot be exaggerated. You were the final and complete sacrifice paid for all. Thank you.*

# Allegiance Gone Awry

They screamed out, "Take him away! Take him away and crucify him!" Pilate replied, "Shall I nail your king to a cross?" The high priests answered, "We have no other king but Caesar!"

JOHN 19:15

The high priests claimed to put their allegiance to Caesar above God. In fact, this may have been very true of them. Though they should have known God best, they sentenced his Son to death on a cross. Their allegiance was not to the Roman Empire but to their own influence within it. They loved their life more than they loved the mercy of God.

The high priests missed out on a key lesson of God's kingdom: "The person who loves his life and pampers himself will miss true life! But the one who detaches his life from this world and abandons himself to me, will find true life and enjoy it forever" (John 12:25). We must be committed to detaching our allegiance from systems of this world that preserve our comfort and instead give ourselves to the leadership of Christ. His ways are life-giving, restorative, and for our good.

*Jesus, you can have my life. I am yours. You have my allegiance and my heart.*

## Crucified

Jesus carried his own cross out of the city to the place called "The Skull," which in Aramaic is Golgotha. And there they nailed him to the cross. He was crucified, along with two others, one on each side with Jesus in the middle.

JOHN 19:17–18

Carrying his own cross out of the city, Jesus bore not just the weight of his looming death but the weight of the world's sins as well. The cross he bore was more than the physical beams that pressed him down and exhausted him physically.

The nails driven into his hands marked the end. There would be no escaping this. Yet escape from death, avoidance of it, was not Jesus' mission. He had to go through it in order to conquer it. Our mortal bodies fail all of us. We cannot escape the deterioration of aging bodies. That is not the promise of Christ. The promise of Christ, the legacy of the Crucified One, is that we will be raised to glory with him in the realm of his eternal kingdom. We should not despise our mortality. Even in our failing health, Jesus sympathizes with us. What a Savior!

*Messiah, thank you for being willing to experience pain, suffering, and death even though you did not deserve it. I am undone by your sacrifice.*

# To the Very End

Mary, Jesus' mother, was standing next to his cross, along with Mary's sister, Mary the wife of Clopas, and Mary Magdalene.

JOHN 19:25

The dear women in Jesus' life were present until the very end. They did not run off or hide away when the going got tough. Perhaps you know such women, the kind who put up with more than they should and graciously show up in the hardest times. They are faithful friends. They cannot be scared off or intimidated by the powers in place. They are the mama bears and the fierce sisters. They are the faithful friends and dependable ones in a crisis.

We must not give in to the idea that women are somehow less valuable than men, even when tradition, society, and misogyny try to steal their worth in our eyes. Women are as worthy of respect, love, and honor as any man among us. The women standing next to Christ's cross were brave, reliable, and fiercely devoted. May we honor these women among us just as Christ does.

*Jesus, your love is better than the world's conditional love. You break down barriers that the world constructs. I follow your ways, Lord, knowing I am as loved as anyone else.*

# Comfort to One Another

When Jesus looked down and saw the disciple he loved standing with her, he said, "Mother, look—John will be a son to you." Then he said, "John, look—she will be a mother to you!" From that day on, John accepted Mary into his home as one of his own family.

JOHN 19:26–27

John did not run away from the suffering of the Savior. He was the only one of the twelve disciples who stood near the cross and witnessed the crucifixion. He stood in solidarity with the women in Christ's life. Jesus had such love in his heart when he looked at his mother and at John. He knew they would need comfort and that they could find it in each other.

There is tremendous comfort in the company of those who understand our loss and pain. John became like a son, and Mary like a mother to him. Psalm 68:5–6 says, "The lonely he makes part of a family." Grief is a very lonely feeling, but even in mourning, Jesus sets the lonely in family. He did it with Mary and John, and he does it with us too. Look around in your sorrow, and you just may find the comfort you need in those closest to you.

*Lord, thank you for the power of communal comfort. Thank you for the comfort I have already known in community. Thank you for the opportunity for even more as I traverse this life.*

# It Is Finished

When he had sipped the sour wine, he said, "It is finished, my bride!" Then he bowed his head and surrendered his spirit to God.

JOHN 19:30

"It is finished." These were the famous last words of Christ on the cross. The culmination of his ministry, the power of his purpose. Everything that Christ had come to do was finished in that moment when he drew his last breath. The finished work of Christ is the salvation of his people, referred to here as his bride.

The completed work of salvation was finished on the cross, and even still, Christ continues to work through his church today to extend the kingdom realm of God on the earth. All the power of God to save us has been poured out. We have only to receive this precious gift through Christ. As we do, the power of his life within us continually revitalizes us and moves us to do the things that please his heart (see Philippians 2:13). Give God the areas that you have been struggling in, and declare, as Christ did on that day, "It is finished." Put your hope in the presence of God and the power of his love to transform you.

*Savior, thank you for doing all that needed to be done to bring the world into your kingdom and to save us. Simply: thank you.*

## Born by the Wound of God

One of the soldiers took a spear and pierced Jesus' side,
and blood and water gushed out.

JOHN 19:34

As blood and water poured out from Jesus' side, it serves as a picture of the cleansing of the Holy Spirit. When a baby is born, both water and blood come forth. On the cross, Jesus birthed his sons and daughters. Isaiah 9:6 refers to Christ as the Father of Eternity. We are born again in Christ. On his cross he died, but he also birthed new life.

Have you ever thought about being born in Christ in this way? The power of his sacrifice is the life he offers you—an overcoming life. As Paul said in Galatians 2:20, "My new life is empowered by the faith of the Son of God who loves me so much that he gave himself for me, dispensing his life into mine!" We have been co-crucified with Christ, and it is his life that lives in us. What a beautiful and powerful reality.

*Messiah, thank you for the power of your life infused within me. I yield to your leadership, to your love, and to the miracle of your salvation. I am yours.*

# Entombed in a Garden

Near the place where Jesus was crucified was a garden, and in the garden there was a new tomb where no one had yet been laid to rest.

JOHN 19:41

Jesus grieved in a garden, he was betrayed in a garden, and he was laid to rest in a garden. A garden is where the birth of humanity happened, and it is where Jesus rose to life again. The full circle of humanity, birth to death to life again, happened within the context of gardens.

May we find renewal and refreshment as we go to the garden of God's goodness. There, he meets with us. He walks with us. He is present. He is alive. The grave of his burial could not keep Jesus entombed. The power of death could not hold him. He overcame sin and death, rising again on the third day. His life brings us life, and he sows beauty into our yielded hearts where he works the soil and produces fruitful bounty.

*Lord, I want to know your refreshing presence as I walk in the gardens of my own life, the places I retreat to in both good times and in hard times. Meet with me.*

# He Rolls Away Stones

Very early Sunday morning, before sunrise, Mary Magdalene made her way to the tomb. And when she arrived she discovered that the stone that sealed the entrance to the tomb was moved away!

JOHN 20:1

After the Sabbath, Mary went early to the tomb of her friend and teacher. When she arrived, she found the heavy tombstone rolled away. This must have been both startling and alarming. She did not know what the open tomb meant. The stone that had covered the tomb was not light. It took more than one man to put it in place. It would not have been easy to remove.

Jesus did not leave his resurrection a mystery. He left evidence, and soon, he would reveal himself. When we're confronted with confusing circumstances that only enhance our anguish instead of assuaging it, we must remember that the presence of God brings clarity. At times we cannot sense the significance of a moment until after more clarity has come. Jesus, the Resurrected One, still rolls heavy stones of constriction and death from our lives. Let's look for where he is.

*Resurrected One, thank you for the power of your love that cannot be held down by anything, not even death. Bring clarity, peace, and focus when I am waiting for more information to unfold. Calm my anxious heart in your presence.*

# He's Gone

She went running as fast as she could to go tell Peter and the other disciple, the one Jesus loved. She told them, "They've taken the Lord's body from the tomb, and we don't know where he is!"

JOHN 20:2

As soon as Mary realized that Jesus' body was no longer in the tomb, she went running to share the news with his disciples. In her distress, she could not understand what had happened to him, so she came to the fastest and easiest conclusion: someone had taken him away.

Has this ever happened to you, that in your distress you made a wrong assumption? This is not a fault. It is just how we are built. We try to make meaning out of the things that happen in life. Some of those conclusions are wrong, and time and evidence will prove them that way. Thankfully, God is gracious with us in our weakness. He does not blame us for our quick reactions. He does, however, calm our anxiety and anguish with his presence and with the truth. The truth does not rush in full of fear, but it creates space and grounds us in love.

*Jesus, when my nervous system is on high alert, rush around me with your pervasive peace and reveal your truth over the situation.*

# Love Outruns Curiosity

Peter and the other disciple jumped up and ran to the tomb to go see for themselves. They started out together, but the other disciple outran Peter and reached the tomb first.

JOHN 20:3–4

John outran Peter when going to the tomb. Peter was curious, but John was full of love. Those who are passionate to know Jesus rather than simply curious about him have the drive to experience his love and power. May we be like those who run to the empty tomb looking for the One we love.

God puts it this way in Jeremiah 29:13: "If you look for me wholeheartedly, you will find me" (NLT). And in Deuteronomy 4:29, it says, "If you search for him with all your heart and soul, you will find him" (NLT). Passion gives energy to our search, and it takes us from a leisurely walk to a sprint. The passionate heart will see, know, and experience God.

*Lord Jesus, you are the one who sparked the flame of love within my heart when you first called me. I will not neglect the passion that drives me to know you more. Pour the fuel of your mercy on the flame of my love, and I will burn brightly for you.*

*Empty Grave*

Peter came behind him and went right into the tomb. He too
noticed the linen cloths lying there, but the burial cloth that had
been on Jesus' head had been rolled up and placed separate
from the other cloths.

JOHN 20:6–7

Peter was not afraid to enter the tomb where they had laid his Savior. In it, he found the evidence of Jesus' resurrection though he still didn't know what to make of it. The linen burial cloths that Jesus had been wrapped in lay in the tomb, and the one that had covered his face was rolled up. The evidence that he had been there remained, but Jesus was nowhere to be found!

When we revisit the graves of those we lost, bones may remain, but their souls have gone. Jesus rose again to life, body and soul. His resurrection life is our hope and our anchor. Jesus has left behind the evidence of his truth, and he reveals himself to those who search him out. He is ever so good, and we can trust him. Let's lean on his wisdom even when the pieces of the puzzle have not quite come together yet.

*Savior, thank you for leaving evidence of your truth for us to uncover. Reveal the greater truth as I look to you.*

# Just One Look

> The other disciple who had reached the tomb first went in, and
> after one look, he believed! For until then they hadn't understood
> the Scriptures that prophesied that he was destined to rise from
> the dead.
>
> JOHN 20:8–9

Like a curtain being pulled back, the revelation of Christ's resurrection came to John as he entered the tomb. Jesus had told them what would happen, and here was the proof right in front of them. This kind of revelation still unfolds in our lives. There are times when we enter a situation and, suddenly, everything is clarified for us. We can see the truth as plain as day.

These are moments of divine unveiling and understanding. They are moments when everything comes together. Just one look and we are undone by the power of Christ's love, his wisdom, and his life. Just one look and we are filled with the wonder of his truth. Just one look and our hearts are overcome by the mercy of God that reaches us where we are.

*Jesus, thank you for revealing yourself and for bringing clarity through truth and experience. I am in awe of you.*

# Broken by Grief

Mary arrived back at the tomb, broken and sobbing. She stooped
to peer inside, and through her tears she saw two angels in
dazzling white robes, sitting where Jesus' body had been laid—
one at the head and one at the feet!

JOHN 20:11–12

Completely heartbroken and grieving, Mary could not
stay away from the last place where she knew Jesus to
be. She longed to be as close to him as possible. What a surprise, then, when she encountered two angels in his tomb!

When you are broken by your own grief, God sends
messengers of comfort to meet you in the place of your loss.
He will not leave you alone in your anguish. He is so much
better than that. Some comforters will be supernatural, while
others come in flesh and blood form. They are our friends
and loved ones. They are those who know the pangs of heartbreak and who also know the truth of breakthrough. Do not
worry; when you are overwhelmed by your grief, God will
send you comfort right when you need it most.

*God of Comfort, I rely on you in every season of the soul. I
need your love to wash over me in my pain and heartbreak. Be
near and send tangible comfort.*

## My Lord

"Dear woman, why are you crying?" they asked.
Mary answered, "They have taken away my Lord,
and I don't know where they've laid him."

JOHN 20:13

Mary did not know where to find her Lord. It is so interesting that this interaction with actual angels reads so casually. She did not fall at their feet. Her heart was so fixated on finding Jesus that nothing else broke through. Nothing else mattered.

Love leads us to incredible lengths. It can become an all-consuming passion. Separation only heightens the feelings of longing. Do you recognize the longing of your own heart in Mary's statement? The dazzling white robes of the angels did not bring her awe or comfort; they meant nothing to her because these angels were not her Lord. Graciously, Jesus does not leave us wanting or waiting long in our search of him. He was just around the corner from Mary, and he is as close to us.

*Lord, I want my heart to burn with passion for you. My deep longing calls out to the deep source of your love. Don't make me wait too long before you wash over me with your presence. I long for you.*

# First to See Him

She turned around to leave, and there was Jesus standing in front of her, but she didn't realize that it was him! He said to her, "Dear woman, why are you crying? Who are you looking for?" Mary answered, thinking he was only the gardener, "Sir, if you have taken his body somewhere else, tell me, and I will go."

JOHN 20:14–15

Clouded by grief, Mary could not focus on what was right before her. Have you ever cried so hard that the world became blurry and your mind was unable to fixate on your surroundings? This is what I imagine Mary experienced. She wanted to find her Savior, and yet here he was, standing right in front of her.

Without fanfare, Jesus walks into our lives and asks us what we are looking for. He asks questions that force us to connect with him. He did not float from the sky when he revealed himself to Mary. Instead, he appeared in a painfully normal way, without pomp and circumstance. We may miss Jesus if we are expecting thunder and lightning. He often speaks in whispers and questions. May we tune in to him and recognize his voice.

*Jesus, you are so kind and patient with us. Open my understanding and the ears and eyes of my heart to recognize you when you speak and move.*

## From Relief to Honor

"Mary," Jesus interrupted her. Turning to face him, she said, "Rabboni!" (Aramaic for "My teacher!") Jesus cautioned her, "Mary, don't cling to me, for I haven't yet ascended to God, my Father. And he's not only my Father and God, but now he's your Father and your God! Now go to my brothers and tell them what I've told you, that I am ascending to my Father—and your Father, to my God—and your God!"

JOHN 20:16–17

At the sound of her name on his lips, Mary instantly recognized the man who was speaking to her. Her relief was palpable. All she had wanted to do was find her teacher, and here he was, standing face-to-face with her once more.

Jesus gave her a precious message—not only for her but for the disciples as well. Jesus called them his brothers for the first time here. Hebrews 2:11 explains this further: "Jesus, the Holy One, makes us holy. And as sons and daughters, we now belong to his same Father, so he is not ashamed or embarrassed to introduce us as his brothers and sisters." We are brothers and sisters with Christ, under the same heavenly Father who loves us. This is more than relief; it is a beautiful mystery and an honor.

*Christ, thank you for making us right with God the Father and for not leaving us alone in this life.*

# Commissioned to Share

Mary Magdalene left to inform the disciples of her encounter with Jesus. "I have seen the Lord!" she told them. And she gave them his message.

JOHN 20:18

Mary was the first one entrusted to carry the gospel message to Jesus' followers. She was given a personal message that was also meant for his friends and brothers. It is important that we recognize the precedent Jesus set with this act. He commissioned Mary, a woman, to share his message with men. In a world that tries to put people in their places, Jesus offered a different way.

We must not be quick to judge the messengers of God. Women are as equipped and capable as men. We must not demean others in the name of God's truth when he came to liberate all in his name and to empower them in his mercy to share his gospel message. No matter who you are, if you have encountered the Lord and been given a message to share, your voice matters. It holds weight. Don't be afraid to share the truth of God's glorious gospel with those you have been sent to. Those God calls he also empowers and equips to do all they need to do.

*Jesus, thank you for commissioning a woman to share your message with the disciples. What a beautiful and empowering precedent!*

# Peace to You

That evening, the disciples gathered together, and because they were afraid of reprisals from the Jewish leaders, they had locked the doors. But suddenly Jesus appeared among them and said, "Peace to you!"

JOHN 20:19

Jesus, appearing behind locked doors to his friends, greeted them by saying, "Peace to you!" His presence was a signal of his lordship, his peace, and his love. Jesus had saved his disciples from raging storms, had fed thousands with a small offering, and had taught them with wisdom, patience, and love. His very presence was sure to be peace to them.

The Prince of Peace still appears to us today through his Spirit. His presence carries a deep, presiding peace. When you are afraid, he will come to you. When you are unsure of how things will turn out, his nearness becomes your strength. As long as he is near, we need not let fear overtake us. He is our courage!

*Prince of Peace, your presence brings deep relief. I rely on your trustworthy leadership and the strength of your love. Fear will not overcome me because your love already has.*

## Overjoyed

*He showed them the wounds of his hands and his side—*
*they were overjoyed to see the Lord with their own eyes!*

JOHN 20:20

Not only does the presence of Jesus bring pervasive peace, but it also brings incredible joy. King David described it this way in Psalm 16:11, "Because of you, I know the path of life, as I taste the fullness of joy in your presence. At your right side I experience divine pleasures forevermore." There is overwhelming joy in the presence of God.

Relief can quickly turn to joy when we are face-to-face with our fulfilled longings. The return of a lost loved one, good news out of a bad diagnosis, and the list goes on. Jesus' resurrection was the culmination of his followers' hopes and the irrefutable truth of Jesus' identity as Messiah. What joy there was, in more ways than one, to celebrate the presence of their Savior! We have as much reason to rejoice today, for Christ is with us through his Spirit. Sing for joy, you redeemed of the Lord!

*Savior, thank you for your presence that brings not only relief but tremendous and overwhelming joy! I worship you, singing your praises and offering you the adoration and devotion of my heart and life.*

## Great Commission

Jesus repeated his greeting, "Peace to you!" And he told them,
"Just as the Father has sent me, I'm now sending you." Then,
taking a deep breath, he blew on them and said, "Receive the Holy
Spirit. I send you to preach the forgiveness of sins—and people's
sins will be forgiven. But if you don't proclaim the forgiveness of
their sins, they will remain guilty."

JOHN 20:21–23

Jesus commissioned his disciples to go and spread the
truth of his gospel. He gave them the Holy Spirit, sending
them to preach the forgiveness of sins. The Spirit would
empower them in all the ways they needed. Without Jesus'
presence, they were not left alone. They were given the
Companion, the One who would continue to teach them,
enable them to walk in Christ's ways, and who would lead
them through their ministries and lives.

The crux of the gospel is the mercy of God extended
through the forgiveness of sins. Without forgiveness, there
is no gospel to tell. God's overwhelming love led Christ to
come to earth in human form, to experience the limitations
of this humanity, all while displaying the power and true
nature of God. Praise be to God that we have been delivered
from sin's grip and set free in the power of his merciful love!

*Jesus, thank you for displaying the nature of God through the
power of your love.*

## What about You?

The disciples informed him, "We have seen the Lord with our own eyes!" Still unconvinced, Thomas replied, "There's no way I'm going to believe this unless I personally see the wounds of the nails in his hands, touch them with my finger, and put my hand into the wound of his side where he was pierced!"

JOHN 20:25

Many of us can probably see ourselves in Thomas' response to the other disciples upon seeing Jesus. He remained skeptical and yet hungry for his own personal encounter. Perhaps it was less skepticism and more the thought of being left out. No matter his heart, Thomas was clear. He wouldn't believe it until he saw his Lord for himself.

Jesus is so very patient with us. He does not require blind belief though he does reward faith. He offers himself to us, meeting us where we are without shame or condemnation. He knows our limitations and our faults, and still he loves us. What gracious mercy he showers us with as he continues to confirm his true identity! Take a step of faith today, no matter how small, even if it feels uncomfortable. Just let it lead you closer to your Savior.

*Jesus, thank you for your patience with me. You are so kind to me. I want my faith to grow stronger in you; help me, Lord.*

## Love Extended

> Looking into Thomas' eyes, he said, "Put your finger here in the wounds of my hands. Here—put your hand into my wounded side and see for yourself. Thomas, don't give in to your doubts any longer, just believe!"
>
> JOHN 20:27

The time had come for Jesus to reveal himself to Thomas. When he did, he offered Thomas his hands and side so Thomas could see, once and for all, that it was truly Jesus standing before him and not some mirage. Gracious and kind, Jesus did not berate Thomas. He did not withhold himself because of Thomas' lack of faith. He still showed up, and he still extended love.

These little gestures of loving-kindness that Jesus displayed add up to a picture of lavish love. This is the mercy of the Father. It is the love that God has for you today, right where you are. Don't let your lack of belief discourage you. He will still make himself known to you. He gives grace upon grace, beloved. He really is that good.

*Gracious Jesus, thank you for being kinder and more patient with me than anyone else has been. Your love is strong, and it blows me away every time I encounter it.*

# Blessed Belief

Jesus responded, "Thomas, now that you've seen me, you believe. But there are those who have never seen me with their eyes but have believed in me with their hearts, and they will be blessed even more!"

JOHN 20:29

Jesus was speaking of you and me when he said, "There are those who have never seen me with their eyes but have believed in me with their hearts." We have not seen him, and yet we love him. We have not touched him, yet he has transformed our hearts with his love. Our belief is to our credit. It is a blessing, in the words of Jesus.

Spend time in the presence of the Lord before you move on with your day. Soak in the knowledge that he knows you, he prays for you, and he blesses you. He is your advocate, your help, and your Savior. More than you can think or imagine—that is what is stored up for you. "He will achieve infinitely more than your greatest request, your most unbelievable dream, and exceed your wildest imagination!" (Ephesians 3:20).

*Jesus, I cannot begin to thank you for all that you have done, are doing, and will continue to do for me. You are wonderful, and I believe in you.*

# Even More Miracles

Jesus went on to do many more miraculous signs in the presence of his disciples, which are not even included in this book.

JOHN 20:30

In the same Spirit in which Jesus continued to do miracles in the presence of his disciples, he still continues to perform miraculous signs today. His power is working in this world. His Spirit has not stopped moving in miraculous mercy. Reflect on ways you have experienced his miraculous work in your own life. How have you seen him move in incredible power, in both little and big ways?

Consider writing some of them down. John wrote a whole book dedicated to the story of Jesus and how Jesus had changed his life. Even so, there was plenty that couldn't fit within the pages of this story—more miracles and wonders. More outrageous love and mercy. This is good news for us. The One who can't be pinned down in one story is the One who continues to move in his people today.

*Miracle Maker, as I recount the ways you have changed my life, I cannot help but see your fingerprints all over the details of my story. How grateful I am, Lord, that you are not finished working yet either.*

# *Never Stop Believing*

All that is recorded here is so that you will fully believe that Jesus is the Anointed One, the Son of God, and that through your faith in him you will experience eternal life by the power of his name!

JOHN 20:31

The testimony of John through this book had one purpose: to increase our faith in Jesus as the Anointed One—not only so that we would believe in him but also with the aim that we would *never stop* believing. How has your faith ebbed and flowed throughout your walk with Christ? Perhaps you have been following Christ for most of your life. Maybe it is still a new journey for you. Wherever this finds you, may you experience encouragement to keep on believing.

The power of God's love is available to you through his Spirit. There is encouragement to help you when your faith is waning. There is strength to empower you when you are weak. All that you need, and so much more, is yours today in Christ.

*Jesus, you are the Anointed One. I will not stop following you, for who is better than you? Only you have the revelation of eternal life. You have the words of life. I am yours.*

## Familiar Places

Later, Jesus appeared once again
to a group of his disciples by Lake Galilee.

JOHN 21:1

Just as Jesus revealed himself in a familiar place to his disciples, so does he reveal himself to us in the ordinary spaces of our lives. There isn't anywhere off-limits to him. His presence is not relegated to a sacred space, such as a church or holy place. He is with us and in us, and that means that wherever we are, there he is too.

Go into your day anticipating Jesus to show up in unexpected ways. He loves to meet us in the places where we have walked together and the places that we go to often. He can meet us as readily in our workplaces as he can in our homes. He can appear to us when we're out at dinner as clearly as he can when we are alone and praying. Let's look for him in these familiar places, for we are sure to find him.

*Lord, I love that you show up in unexpected places and in unforeseen ways. No one can put you in a box, and for that I'm grateful. Encounter me in the ordinary parts of my day. I am expectant.*

# Gone Fishing

Peter told them, "I'm going fishing." And they all replied, "We'll go with you." So they went out and fished through the night, but caught nothing.

JOHN 21:3

Peter was a fisherman by trade before Jesus called him as his follower. It was familiar and comfortable for him— perhaps therapeutic, as well—to go fishing. Together with some of his fellow disciples and friends, he went to do what he knew how to do.

When life takes a turn and we don't know what to do with ourselves, what are the familiar things we go back to? Perhaps we think we can go back to the old life, doing the same things as before. Except when we are changed, we realize that what used to satisfy no longer feed us in the same way. An empty net can feel frustrating after a night of trying our hardest. Thankfully, Jesus is just off the shore, waiting to bring us abundance and direction.

*Jesus, thank you for your persistent presence. Thank you for the power of your transformative love in my life. Do what only you can do, especially when all I know to do falls flat and doesn't work anymore.*

# When Things Don't Work Out

At dawn, Jesus was standing there on the shore, but the disciples didn't realize that it was him! He called out to them, saying, "Hey guys! Did you catch any fish?" "Not a thing," they replied.

JOHN 21:4–5

After a night on the water, the disciples hadn't caught a thing. This wasn't normal, seeing as how they were skilled fisherman. And yet it was true. Can you think of a time when you did all you knew to do and things just didn't turn out as they should have? Thankfully, even when we are out of resources and options, God is not.

The One who created you calls out to you in your barrenness and frustration. He makes his presence known. He won't leave you high and dry. When you have reached the end of yourself—your knowledge, resources, and strength—the Lord offers you his own. Paul said in 2 Corinthians 12:10, "My weakness becomes a portal to God's power." What thresholds are open in your own life? These are opportunities for God's power to shine through.

*Faithful One, you are reliable and true in all that you do. I cannot think of anyone more faithful. Thank you for meeting me in my weakness and giving me your strength.*

# More Than They Could Handle

Jesus shouted to them, "Throw your net over the starboard side,
and you'll catch some!" And so they did as he said, and they
caught so many fish they couldn't even pull in the net!

JOHN 21:6

The power of God provided more than the fishermen could imagine, more than the disciples could handle. Out of a fruitless night, they simply put the nets on the other side, as Jesus instructed, and they were overloaded with fish. This was a miracle!

When God sees us floundering in our need, he does not leave us empty-handed. He gives us instructions, and as we follow them, our need turns into a bounty of blessing. Only God can do this, and he is so gracious to do it. Barrenness is not our destiny. Though we may struggle to make headway for a night season, when Christ shows up, he brings overwhelming blessing, above and beyond our need, to astound us with his kindness.

*God, I believe that you have not forgotten me. You know my struggles and my needs, and you will provide a bounteous blessing. I trust you.*

## *Revelatory Realizations*

The disciple whom Jesus loved said to Peter, "It's the Lord!" When Peter heard him say that, he quickly wrapped his outer garment around him, and because he was athletic, he dove right into the lake to go to Jesus!

JOHN 21:7

Recognizing a miracle of Jesus when it happened, John realized that the man who had directed them from the shore was none other than their beloved Lord. Peter could not contain his excitement, nor did he have the patience to wait until the boat pulled ashore. He jumped right into the water and swam to meet Jesus.

When revelation hits us, bringing awe, wonder, and understanding, how do we react? Do we rush into the water like Peter? Do we recognize the work of God and share it with others? Whatever our reactions, the Lord is the same. He waits for us to turn to him. What was the last thing that caused you to turn to Jesus in wonder?

*Lord, when you move, I am moved. I am overwhelmed by your goodness when you provide in extravagant ways. It's unbelievable, really, your love for me. I turn to you today.*

# Bring What You Caught

When they got to shore, they noticed a charcoal fire with some roasted fish and bread. Then Jesus said, "Bring some of the fish you just caught."

JOHN 21:9–10

Jesus prepares a fire, and he also asks us to bring what we have to share. Jesus provided the fish; he told them where to put their nets. And yet the fish became an offering and a shared meal for them. The same is true in our lives. God provides for us, and as we come to him, we get to bring back to him some of what he gives.

What do you have to bring to Christ today? What do you have to share with him? Think about what he has done in your life, what he has offered you and blessed you with. Out of the bounty, there is something to share with him. It will nourish you both as you bring it to him. Jesus has made a fire for you, and he wants to share a meal with you today. What will you bring?

*Jesus, thank you for all that you have provided for me. Thank you for what you have helped me with. I bring you what I have today. We can share it together.*

# God's Blessing Doesn't Destroy

Peter waded into the water and helped pull the net to shore. It was full of many large fish, exactly one hundred and fifty-three, but even with so many fish, the net was not torn.

JOHN 21:11

When Peter went to pull the net to shore, the net was not torn even though there were copious fish in it. The blessing of God does not bring destruction. It preserves, brings life, and restores. It is not a burden but a relief and a gift. It is pure love poured out in miraculous ways.

In this world, gifts often come with a cost. They may benefit some and destroy others. Jesus' blessings do not work this way. There is no downside to his generosity. He does not withhold from some in order to pour out upon others. He is the same generous, kind, and good God to everyone. In light of this reality, we can receive what he offers and bless others in the same way.

*Life-Giver, thank you for bringing life in all you do. You preserve what seems to be impossible under the weight of your blessing. Thank you. May my generosity reflect yours.*

## Come, Eat

"Come, let's have some breakfast," Jesus said to them. And not one of the disciples needed to ask who it was, because every one of them knew it was the Lord.

JOHN 21:12

Jesus invites you to dine with him today. Around the breakfast table, he longs to break bread with you and connect. He knows what will nourish us, body, soul, and spirit. He has all that we long for. He restores us with kindness just as he restored Peter around the coals. His forgiveness is not just a lofty ideal; it is present and practical.

Is there someone you have been meaning to reach out to? A relationship that you want to restore? Consider inviting them to a meal. Over the table, share your heart with them. Share a meal with them. Even if they walk away unchanged in their heart, at least they will be fed.

*Merciful Jesus, you displayed so much connection over the sharing of meals. May I not neglect the fellowship and power of breaking bread together. Thank you for providing for my physical needs and for connecting with my heart. You are so good.*

## Still Serving

Jesus came close to them and served them the bread and the fish. This was the third time Jesus appeared to his disciples after his resurrection.

JOHN 21:13–14

Even after his death and resurrection, Jesus didn't stop serving his disciples. Beloved, he still serves us as well. He is such a beautiful and tender leader. He doesn't require that we do anything he wouldn't do himself. We will never grow out of the necessity to serve others in love because love shows itself in actions.

John explained this concept further in his epistle: "Beloved children, our love can't be an abstract theory we only talk about, but a way of life demonstrated through our loving deeds. We know that the truth lives within us because we demonstrate love in action" (1 John 3:18–19). If we want to reveal the love of God living within us, then we have to live it out in practice, and acts of service are one way that this happens. How can you serve others in practical love today?

*Jesus, your loving leadership is such a clear example of how to live, love, and lead. I want to follow in your footsteps, my Lord.*

## Acts of Love

After they had breakfast, Jesus said to Peter, "Simon, son of Jonah, do you burn with love for me more than these?" Peter answered, "Yes, Lord! You know that I have great affection for you!" "Then take care of my lambs," Jesus said.

JOHN 21:15

Peter learned a hard lesson through his denial of Jesus: that he was capable of turning on the One he loved. Gone was his overly self-assured attitude about his faith. He was humbled greatly. Still, his love for Jesus had not diminished; only his self-righteousness had. When he ran out of the boat to Jesus, he was running toward the One he depended on. Jesus did not disappoint. He restored him and reassured him.

In this loving exchange between Jesus and Peter, there was a question of devotion, followed by a call to action. "If you love me…then take care of my lambs." Have you ever felt the question that Jesus posed to Peter? If you love Christ, then he has ways for you to show your deep affection through acts of love toward others. It always works this way. Love for God extends to love for people. How can you show your love for God to others today?

*Jesus, I love you so much more than I can say, so I will show you with my actions.*

# Keep Following

(Jesus said this to Peter as a prophecy of what kind of death he would die, for the glory of God.) And then he said, "Peter, follow me!"

JOHN 21:19

E ven in the face of certain suffering, which none of us can escape in this life anyway, will we choose to keep following the Lord? Pain is not a punishment; it is a part of life in this fallen world. Jesus does not call us to easy lives; that was never his promise. He sets us free from the bondage of sin and eliminates death's power over us by ushering us into eternal life in his kingdom. These are promises that he cannot break. Jesus has offered us peace with God. What greater gift could there be?

Jesus is worth following. His leadership is unlike any other, and his love is unmatched. He offers us grace upon glorious grace, filling us up with the fullness of himself. There is no better person to hitch our lives to, no one more merciful or kinder. He is powerful, moving in miraculous signs and following through in faithfulness to his Word. Keep following him, beloved, for he came to "give you everything in abundance...life in its fullness until you over-flow!" (John 10:10).

*Holy Lord, I choose to follow you not out of obligation but out of sheer gratitude and devotion. You are worthy of my trust.*

## Eyes Focused

When Peter saw [John], he asked Jesus, "What's going to happen to him?" Jesus replied, "If I decide to let him live until I return, what concern is that of yours? You must still keep on following me!"

JOHN 21:21–22

If we become fixated on what God does through others, it is a distraction from what God wants to do in our own lives. Jesus leads us uniquely, for each of our paths will take a different shape. He does not ask us to follow him so that our lives will look like someone else's. We must look to *him* and not become distracted by what he is leading others into.

Where has your focus been? Has it been on Christ, the One who leads you? He has grace enough for each of us in abundant measure. Don't let comparison steal your focus. It is a trap that can lead to disenchantment and bitterness. When we follow Christ, we trust him to do what is best for us, to help us through every twist and turn, and most of all, we have the power of his presence. He is good to all, and he blends his tender love into everything he does.

*Loving Lord, I trust you to guide me into your goodness. Help me to keep my eyes fixed on you and to not be distracted by comparison. Thank you.*

# More Than Can Be Recorded

Jesus did countless things that I haven't included here. And if every one of his works were written down and described one by one, I suppose that the world itself wouldn't have enough room to contain the books that would have to be written!

JOHN 21:25

If we were to write down all the things that God has done—the wonders of his goodness and mercy, the many miracles, and the answers to prayer—the world could not contain the books it would take. John said this two thousand years ago. How much truer that is today, for God has not stopped moving!

Think through your own life, even over the last year. Write down all the things that come to mind when you consider God's hand in it. What has Jesus done for you? How has he come through for you? As you write them down, remember that these are just a few examples of his faithfulness. There is so much more where that came from! When you are finished, offer him praise for his goodness, and worship him from an overflowing heart of gratitude. As you look ahead to this next year, go into it with expectation and hope. He is still moving, and he is faithful.

*Glorious One, thank you for all that you have done for me. I am in awe of your powerful love in my life. I worship you.*

Brian Simmons is the lead translator of The Passion Translation®. The Passion Translation (TPT) is a heart-level translation that uses Hebrew, Greek, and Aramaic manuscripts to express God's fiery heart of love to this generation, merging the emotion and life-changing truth of God's Word. The hope for TPT is to trigger inside every reader an overwhelming response to the truth of the Bible and to reveal the deep mysteries of the Scriptures in the love language of God, the language of the heart. Brian is currently translating the Old Testament.

After a dramatic conversion to Christ in 1971, Brian and his wife, Candice, answered the call of God to leave everything behind and become missionaries to unreached peoples. Taking their three children to the tropical rain forest of Central America, they planted churches for many years with the Paya-Kuna people group. Brian established